SLAVIC WITCHCRAFT

"Natasha Helvin has not shied away from including both blessings and curses in a comprehensive Slavic grimoire that addresses just about any life situation. Within these fascinating pages you will learn to craft love spells and breakup spells, spells for money and business success, spells to win in court, to surround yourself with protection while traveling, spells for peace in the home, for health and healing, and for prophetic dreams. The author concludes with traditional Slavic tips for how to live a good life. A very practical how-to guidebook for anyone interested in ancient forms of peasant wisdom and magic."

Ellen Evert Hopman, author of
The Real Witches of New England
and *The Sacred Herbs of Samhain*

"*Slavic Witchcraft* is a deep dive into the spells and practices of traditional witches from Russia, Ukraine, and Belarus. Natasha Helvin shares cultural and familial practices—real old world witchcraft—that can't be found in any other modern book on the subject. This book reveals the ancient pagan practices that are still entwined with the current Orthodox religion that is very much in place."

Phoenix LeFae, author of *Cash Box Conjure: Hoodoo Spells for Luck and Money*
and *Hoodoo Shrines and Altars*

"In *Slavic Witchcraft,* Natasha Helvin offers us a fine selection of Slavic charms arranged by type—love, money, protection, health, and more. Her book reflects ancestral beliefs that Christianity and the demonization of former deities were unable to eradicate. This book is definitely worth going out of your way to get."

Claude Lecouteux, former professor of medieval literature and civilization at the Sorbonne and author of *The Book of Grimoires*

SLAVIC WITCHCRAFT

Old World Conjuring Spells and Folklore

NATASHA HELVIN

DESTINY BOOKS

Destiny Books
Rochester, Vermont

Destiny Books
One Park Street
Rochester, Vermont 05767
www.DestinyBooks.com

Destiny Books is a division of Inner Traditions International

Cataloging-in-Publication Data for this title is available from the Library of Congress

ISBN 978-1-62055-842-3 (print)
ISBN 978-1-62055-843-0 (ebook)

Printed and bound in the United States by McNaughton & Gunn, Inc.

10 9 8 7 6 5 4

Text design and layout by Debbie Glogover
This book was typeset in Garamond Premier Pro with Mackay, Gill Sans MT Pro, and ITC Legacy Sans used as display fonts

To send correspondence to the author of this book, mail a first-class letter to the author c/o Inner Traditions • Bear & Company, One Park Street, Rochester, VT 05767, and we will forward the communication, or contact the author directly at **info@worldofconjuring.com**.

This book is dedicated to my roots and my ancestors. Thank you Granny, thank you Mom, and thank you to my dear sister for your inspiration and help with this book. Thank you all for keeping the tradition alive for many generations in our family and for passing it down to me and my children.

In memory of my beloved mother.

Contents

A Cautionary Note to the Reader

Slavic witchcraft is cerebral and philosophical, a studied practice of intellectual arts and manifestation of the human Will. It is for those who are curious about the unknown, rather than those who fear mysteries and taboos. Witchcraft favors the bold, and it attracts the most driven and motivated of the intelligentsia.

This book is intended for readers who seek to make changes in their lives and embrace the mysterious and the forbidden. This resource is a little gem for people who want to learn about Russian folklore, magic, and beliefs with measurable results—or who are just curious about East Slavic people.

Any reader who uses or tries to use any of the spells from this book does so entirely at their own risk. The author and the publisher accept no liability if the work does or does not have the desired effect or results. This book is for educational, spiritual, and inspirational use only.

INTRODUCTION

Sorcery as a Living Tradition

Storms make trees take deeper roots.

Dolly Parton

Russian sorcery is based on the interventions of gods, spirits, and forces of nature in the lives of common people, as well as the ability to control these forces. I can say with certainty that Russians have used sorcery to achieve their goals for many centuries.

Magic was an integral part of pagan traditions practiced by our ancestors, and that magic had as its aim help in life, healing, and freedom from negative energy. Our ancestors used magic of all kinds—from spells and charms to incantations for luck in business and battles.

Russian sorcery is a synthesis of paganism and Christianity. There are still people who celebrate pagan festivals and conjure on Christian holy days. There are still witches who whisper upon tied knots to curse or heal.

Sorcerers are capable of some truly extraordinary things.

I was born in the Soviet state and lived there until I was eighteen years old. As a child, I saw my grandmother and mother use magic in their everyday lives to help neighbors, friends, and others seeking help. I am a fifth-generation hereditary witch, on both my maternal and paternal sides. In my family we never separated magic from everyday life. My mother, sister, and I held a séance to contact the deceased when I was seven years old. We read tarot cards to see if we would pass a school test or if a boy I liked would ask me on a date. Every "Christian" holiday was a great time for me and my sister, as we performed many divinations in a way that was fun, playful, and appropriate for our ages. We called on the spirits of the dead in so many different ways, and it was just a part of our fun time with family.

I learned from my family the ancient secrets of magic and healing and the boundless potential of the human spirit, and I inherited my passion for magic and fortune-telling from them. From this long line of metaphysicians and rich spiritual cultural heritage, the roots of occultism and conscious thinking rapidly developed in me at a very young age.

What we believe in is the ability to change the world by starting from within yourself. We believe that you can bring forth peace by first learning to love and appreciate yourself and your ancestors. We believe that rules are not arbitrary but instead made by you in accordance with your own beliefs. We believe in free will. And we believe in magic and the power that it holds! We adhere to the wisdom of our own voices, because we know the greatest gift in the universe is free will—ultimate and omnipotent—bound only by love and ameliorated by the practice of magic.

Each one of us is an epicenter of self-empowerment because we make our own rules rather than wishing for a nonexistent guidebook to life. You don't need the permission of a self-help guru to go out and conquer the world. You have all the potential that you need within you to take charge of your life, to learn the fundamentals of true powers of conjuring, and to love without condition or expectation of reciprocity. We embrace free thought and celebrate the forbidden as part of our spiritual independence!

My childhood and teenage years were fulfilled by magic; magic was everywhere in the air, in everything we did, in the way my parents spoke and acted on a daily basis. For us it wasn't magic; for us it was the way we lived, and we didn't know anything else, so it was normal. From the time I left my birthplace until now, every single day I miss that kind of magic in the air. Living without magic is like returning from vacation to work you dislike, going back to the routine and (for most people) the normal way of life.

What made me write this book? If I can say it in one word: nostalgia. Nostalgia for real freedom—the one found in magic, not the artificially presented one. I wanted to share and show people that there is another life out there, in the rural areas of my country—and I'm sure many other countries as well—where there are still believers in the old ways and people who live their life freely: free from the dogma, rules, and grime of the modern world.

❋

In this book, I will explain the secrets of the profound system of thoughts and practices that underlie the East Slavic culture. Both the spiritual heritage of ancient beliefs and the practical steps that we can take to help ourselves in our daily lives are presented in this book.

I begin by explaining the relationship between Christianity and paganism in Russia, as I know it from my parents, grandparents, and the community around us. The foundation of our upbringing there is magic: in bedtime stories, movies, and literature; at school (folklore); in magical proverbs, and more. The core message is that you can do and achieve anything if you believe in yourself.

I will also give some background on Slavic magic—what it is, why it works, and some folklore about sorcerers that persists to this day.

Next are several chapters on spells. These spells are mostly from my family; some spells were collected from different people while I was traveling abroad and going on expeditions to rural areas of Russia. The spells are divided into the categories of love and relationships; money, wealth, and business; protection; house and home; health and healing; and dreams and divinations.

Cemeteries are their own special magic, and I have included a chapter on cemetery traditions, folklore, and spells.

The book concludes with Slavic magic tips for all occasions.

1 Pagan Christianity or Christian Paganism

Russians brought Christianity and paganism together to the extent that it is difficult to say which one has prevailed. Christianity—accepted within itself the pagan origins, or paganism, which swallowed up the Christian dogma.

CARDINAL HÉLIE DE TALLEYRAND-PÉRIGORD, FOURTEENTH CENTURY (IN ONE OF HIS LETTERS TO POPE JOHN XXII)

In Russia, Christianity and paganism constantly struggled with each other to dominate the popular consciousness, but in an odd way these two belief systems also complemented each other. The baptism of Russia happened forcefully. In fact, there were three separate attempts to convert Russia to Christianity, and they all failed. People didn't want to accept a new faith that was significantly different from paganism, and with good reason. Authorities were trying to manipulate the most sacred and intimate thing a person has: his faith. Christian saints began to replace pagan gods, but the old gods were always there, hiding underneath.

This led to the creation of a unique "dual faith" phenomenon that still persists. There is no reason to categorize the mixture as good or bad. Its existence simply shows the originality and uniqueness of

Russian culture. To this day, every part of our lives is infused with the remnants of paganism, even though more than a thousand years have passed! That's how persistent a religion can be.

BELIEFS OF THE OLD FAITH

Old Believers or Original Believers refer to people who lived in the time of the ancient Slavs. It was a huge tribe that inhabited not only the contemporary territory of the Old Believers of Russia, Ukraine, and Belarus but also of the Balkans and Baltic states. They worshipped the old gods and brought them rich offerings in return for peace and a good harvest.

The ancient Slavs performed the rites that formed the basis of today's elemental and natural magic. The four elements represented pure nature for all Old Believers. It was nature that fortified their magic and combined the strength of all the elements at once.

Earth, mother, protector. She gave food, clothes, and the ability to sow and harvest crops.

Water, without which there would be no crops. A human cannot live without water; plants and animals need it every day. The Slavs settled along the rivers not only for their crops but also in search of protection. Crossing a stormy river is not an easy task, so their cities were all well protected on one side.

Air is no less essential than water.

Fire gives us warmth, light, and protection from wild animals. With fire, it was possible not only to cook food and warm your home but also to make weapons. By then, Slavs had already mastered metalworking.

In addition to the elements, there are several generations of Slavic pagan gods. The first, and the oldest, begins with the god of thunder named Perun. The god of the earth, waters, and the Underworld is Veles. The solar deity is Dazhboga. The god named Rod preserved the sacred connection between generations because the power of all the ancestors lies in the hands of the one who honors his ancestral history, knows the names of his grandfathers, and honors their religion; this is a foundational belief of Slavic pagans. Women got help and relief during difficult childbirth with the support of the goddesses Lada and Mokosh.

Many centuries later, in Perun's place came Jarilo—a wise, fair, but very warlike god. It was at this time that a division happened. Whole provinces that refused to recognize the new gods appeared. They didn't want to betray the faith of their homeland and their grandfathers. The Old Believers wanted to continue their rituals in honor of Perun, but the followers of the new gods argued that the future lies with Jarilo, god of the Sun, Light, and Power.

The Old Believers' faith was bound tightly to their magic and rituals. The majority of spells that originate in that Slavic period come to us from the era of the oldest pagan gods. The great Slavic magic that drew its power from nature was born in this period. Their lives were full of mysticism, rituals, spells. And it came from both white and dark sources.

In these ancient times Nature and Destiny were ruthless to men. They needed both types of magic to survive. Back then, the balance between dark and white magic was much stronger. Sorcerers helped people to choose the right time to plant crops and build. They also blessed their exploits and battles. The Old Believers had many enemies, but they also had many friends. Their gods always stood side by side, reminding their followers of their presence with thunderclaps, rain, bright sunlight, or fertile soil.

CONVERSION TO ORTHODOX CHRISTIANITY

Prince Vladimir brought Christianity to his people from the Byzantine Empire (known as Eastern Christianity) about 988 to 990 CE. Pagan temples were crushed, idols burned, and traditions forgotten. However, these changes only took place in public.

After the conversion of Kievan Rus, Christianity and paganism started to exist simultaneously, seemingly in parallel. The new religion did not automatically exclude the former; the two religions even

Fig. 1.1. Yan Vyshatich—an eleventh-century Kievan nobleman and military commander—and pagans. Behind Yan Vyshatich is a priest carrying a cross. The pagans are wearing the traditional clothing containing symbols of the gods. Painting by Sergey Ivanov, 1912.

began to be consolidated. Paganism proved so difficult to overcome that Christianity had to adopt some of its features. At the beginning of the thirteenth century it became common for baptized individuals to continue to observe pagan traditions and rites, believe in ghost and spirits, and worship pagan gods, only sometimes in secret.

Modern Orthodox Christian icons are modified pagan idols; and in depictions of some Orthodox saints, it's often possible to recognize features of pagan gods. Similarly, there were many existing holy days among the ancient Slavs in close connection with the harvest, fertility, and good weather that the church co-opted by converting them to their Christian holy days. Sometimes this changed the dates; sometimes the dates coincided. Holidays dedicated to pagan gods (Kupala, for example) thus became the feast days of Christian saints. This was to help sorcerers to survive and not be killed or tortured by "the Christians."

The day of Perun's festival coincided with the veneration of Elijah the prophet, so Perun became Elijah—who, according to local belief, rode a chariot across the sky during thunderstorms. Veles was replaced by Saint Nicholas, one of the most revered saints in Russia, as well as Saint George. The Cult of the Mother merged with that of the Virgin Mary, mother of God; while Dazhboga took on the guise of Christ. Meanwhile, Mokosh evolved into Saint Parascheva of the Balkans, whose icons were placed at springs or fountains. As for the lower deities, the attitude toward them became increasingly negative with time. They gradually became demons or simply malevolent beings in the eyes of the public.

Pagans who didn't want to be baptized were fleeing into the woods and killing priests. Tensions rose until riots broke out. And there were many pagan rebellions! But the empire's policy, even if it was forced, wasn't barbarous. The government used patient, well-thought-out tactics to bring about conversion, and in the end its efforts were successful. But the new religion was unstable, lacking the deep roots that paganism had.

As proof, in the second part of the eleventh century, Russia was struck with crop failure and famine. Christianity couldn't remedy such a situation, because it wasn't said to rule the forces of nature. But pagan rites and rituals, which were mostly bound to natural phenomena, could. As a result, the reverse movement began, and people sought to return to their roots. The church brutally repressed the movement, altering the situation to its own benefit—as it has done repeatedly since.

SACRIFICIAL OBJECTS: OFFERINGS

An offering is the most basic way to communicate with the gods in paganism. In Orthodox Christianity, an offering holds a completely different meaning, but it is still a part of Christianity that resembles pagan custom. As a rule, offerings take the form of gifts. These gifts are used to seal a promise, make a request, or give thanks for a miracle that has already taken place, such as the miracle of healing. These are known as voluntary gifts.

The practice of offerings in Christianity in general, and in Orthodox Christianity in particular, is considered by many to be a direct legacy of paganism. As an example, we can observe the practice of adorning icons with various pieces of jewelry. The icons are made with golden and silver pieces and are often even bejeweled with precious stones. Then people decorate them with crosses, women's jewelry such as earrings and bracelets, and rings and other finery. Some people also hang offerings on the icons. During the rule of Peter I, the church attempted to root out this practice, but it remains. However, there is one method of giving offerings that has died out, possibly due to its direct connections with paganism. This is the practice of gifting icons with jewelry made to represent an image of a part of the human body, or of the person as a whole. If your eye, arm, or leg is injured, you could go to the local monastery and order a silver replica or symbol of the corresponding part of the body. You would then sew onto the icon a prayer for recovery or one to show gratitude.

Some feel that the lit candles used by parishioners in church or lit in front of icons are also sacrificial gifts. It's safe to assume that the practice of lighting the candles and lamps is also inherited from paganism, in connection with sacrificial bonfires.

SIMILARITIES WITH VOODOO

Slavic paganism is unique, but it does share some features with another religion: Voodoo. Voodoo is a religion created by the descendants of African ethnic groups who were enslaved and brought to the Americas and later Christianized by missionaries. Voodoo, like Slavic paganism, has aspects of the older African religions but with Christian aspects incorporated or overlaid. Importantly, both Voodoo and Slavic paganism honor ancestors at their cores. In addition, the magical aspects of Slavic paganism and Voodoo are similar in the way practitioners create and work with spells. Another similarity is that when we create work we call upon outside powers such as spirit, demon, soul of the dead person; in Voodoo they create work and call upon an outside power as well, in this case spirit, god, lwa, or the soul of a dead person.

2

Slavic Magic, Power, and Sorcery

MAGICAL WORDS

At the beginning, there was a word. And the word was *magic.* Yes, creating matter from nothing with only the verbal expression of your will is a work of magic. A word is energy and power. With words we can kill or give a new life. In the real world, empires are run by words, laws are laid down, armies are built, treaties are signed, wedding vows are exchanged, and feelings are expressed.

In our world we can acquire various treasures. We can request them from our patrons or order them from those beneath us. But we must remember that the great powers here on Earth are not the most important powers in the universe. There are more significant figures, forces of nature and gods who are able to give us what we want or take away what we already have. Direct verbal contact with these forces is the most ancient type of magic.

But of course—the use of ordinary words and expressions is unlikely to help you establish contact with the center of the universe. Instead, you must use the special verbal formulas that we call sorcerer's spells and magical incantations.

The words in incantations have multiple meanings. You can use them to command, ask persistently, or beseech for the sake of something. You can even use them to bring change to yourself. The simplest kind of incantation is to directly address the object you wish to influence. You can use this spell to influence people, current or future events, and unknown objects. You can even influence personified natural phenomena by addressing them as you would living creatures.

As a rule, such appeals are in the form of commands, demands, and orders. They are distinguished by an imperative tone, and often, there is mention made of punishment in case of failure to deliver the requirements. The basic formula for such incantations is "I command you to do this and that . . . and if you do not, death and destruction await you."

The second incantation formula consists of incantations that are addressed not toward the object of influence but toward the mediator, or the Higher Powers, from which the aid is expected. You address them to ancient gods, to the sun, the moon, the stars, various elements of nature, the spirits of your ancestors, or toward various astral entities, whose powers can solve this or that problem. Often those kinds of incantations are conducted with real or symbolic offerings. In this case, they are constructed as a two-phrase formula: "From me to you . . . from you to me."

Also, the distinguishing feature of any incantation is the mention of a third, more powerful force that reigns over the power you are invoking. It must be a force whose fury the addressee will fear, or a force who appears as an authority, both in the human world and in the world of shadows. "I conjure thee in the name of the Lord Almighty . . . I conjure thee by the force of the west wind . . . In the name and glory of the Angel of light and darkness, I conjure you to do . . . etc."

The original meaning of the words *spell* and *hex* was "speak onto." Traditionally, you must say spells directly onto the things and objects you are using so that your breath reaches their surface. Essentially, this is a direct transfer of magical power and energy to a material object. Spells are usually spoken onto Fire, Earth, Water, and Air (on the wind); onto drinks, food, and spices (salt, sugar, pepper); onto the injured part of a sick person or animal; onto things that belong to the person you wish to influence in a certain way, or the objects needed to achieve your desires.

There are spells used to join or connect two existing phenomena. Such spells are constructed according to the formula "As . . . so," "When . . . then" and are very often meant to coincide with unique natural processes. For example, "When all the leaves from this tree have fallen, then the disease shall pass." The forces of nature that are responsible for certain processes can also be invoked for other purposes.

By rule, "joining spells" are said at the same time as actions that imitate what is supposed to happen. They describe and explain the imitative actions, and thus determine their true direction. For example, a sorcerer lights a candle and says, "I light not the candle, but kindle love. As the flame is vivid and bright, so will love be vivid and bright."

At the same time, a huge number of spells exist that are said without any accompanying action or material objects. In these cases, the spell replaces the real action with a mental representation of the events described. Thus, the power of words in a spell is limitless. They can rule elements; prevent or bring forth rain, thunder, and storms; ensure a plentiful harvest or make fields and gardens barren; expand herds or exterminate them with a plague; give a person success and happiness or send disaster and misfortunes upon them; drive illness away from the sick or transfer sickness to the healthy; kindle love in someone's heart or extinguish their passion; awaken the feeling of mercy and meekness or bitterness and anger in judges and superiors; make a weapon's aim true or make a warrior invulnerable; staunch blood; turn humans to animals and animals into trees and stones. In this manner, magical words can manipulate any event, alter objects at their core, and bend all the influences of god and nature to the caster's will.

MAGICAL ACTIONS

A magic work or a magic ritual is a construction of astral spiritual forms, a framework for future events. The building material for this framework is the energy of natural elements such as Earth, Fire, Water, and Air, and the tool for its construction is your will, faith, and imagination.

When you begin the magic ritual, you will enter a special spiritual state that is separate from daily moods and thoughts. Use your will, faith, and imagination. As you perform the ritual, envision the events your actions will bring about. Be completely certain of your righteousness and that of what you are doing. You must believe that the events you need to come to pass will surely happen in your life. Treat the future as if it is already occurring in the present.

When you perform the actions required by a spell, you must "see" the consequences they will have. During an incantation, surround yourself with symbols and images of the forces you invoke and the events you desire. If you're using the forces of fire, water, moon, space, or other earthly and higher spheres, then their images must be visibly present in your sorcery space, whether in familiar forms or in the form of symbols and ambiguous visions born from your subconscious.

Your will must aid your faith and imagination. It must steer the energy, yours or any other, in the right direction, create a pressured space or vacuum, move the items, and move hands on the clock to the time that you need. Your sorcerer's will acts like a lens to focus your emotions and forces; it helps you reach the goals you've chosen and achieve what you envision.

When you carry out magical changes in real space, you'll be using not only your internal but also your external forces and energies. Just as in the physical world, different materials are needed to produce different things and objects. Energies of different qualities are used in a spiritual plane. The basic materials from which all the objects in the physical world are built are the four elements of nature: Earth, Water, Fire, and Air. Aspects of these main forces of nature (their energy) are present in all manifestations of our reality and continuously exert various influences in every part of our life. This is why the correct detection and use of the energy of the four nature elements is extremely necessary for those who decide to change the world and themselves.

The world surrounding us is fraught with other spatial influences and energies that can be useful for building the reality you want. First among them is the energy of the nearest stars and planets, such as the moon, the sun, Venus, Jupiter, Mars, Saturn, and Mercury. All these celestial objects, as well as the gods in whose honor they were named, are the patrons of certain human activities. Therefore, their influence is used in specific cases and under certain circumstances. It is necessary to appeal to the Patronage of Higher Powers to have a reliable defense and a good opportunity to control what is happening around you.

After completing the magic, do not settle for what you've achieved.

Continue using magic for the rest of your life. Remember that magic is not only those ritual and ceremonial actions but is also ever present in everyday life. Do not be afraid of possible small failures and difficulties. When you are striving for something great, errors cannot be avoided. If something doesn't work out the first time, trying again or approaching the problem from a different direction will certainly lead you to success. Remember that a lot depends solely on you, on the decisions and promises that you make. You will feel a secret bond with everything that lives on the planet and exists in this endless universe. You will make your own choices and learn not only about the obvious, everyday world but also about its hidden possibilities.

TALISMANS AND AMULETS

Every physical object contains internal energy that was given to it from nature or that it received as a result of some actions. This energy has constant influence over space and other objects. It's safe to say that we live in a world of continuous interactions and energy exchanges. Our physical and spiritual states depend a great deal on what kind of objects we communicate with each day and what energy we get from them—our abilities and qualities, our external and internal attractiveness, and many other things that precisely determine our role and position on the physical plane. Thus, by choosing particular objects for our environment, we can somewhat influence our destiny. This act is magic itself. For the fastest and most effective result, you should choose the most active objects that are intended for magical transformations by nature itself or created by human hands for this purpose.

Items that are rich with energy are called talismans or amulets. It should be noted that in different countries and at different times the terms *talisman* and *amulet* have had different interpretations and meanings.

The word *talisman* comes from Arabic *tilism* or *tilsam,* which translates as "magic image" or "magic letter." These were originally labels for special objects with secret inscriptions and magic symbols. Talismans were made from stone, metal, and wood, but most often it was just an ordinary piece of parchment covered with letters and images. These symbols, in the form of magic spells, were supposed to protect the owner of the talisman from various misfortunes or fulfill his desires. (The most famous of the ancient talismans is the so-called Abracadabra.) Over time, the word *talisman* began to represent other objects of the material world that carry the properties of those ancient pieces of parchment.

It is believed that a talisman supports and enhances the personal abilities and qualities given to a person by nature. It creates an inner harmony between the person and the world around him and helps him to withstand and counter troubles and difficulties. So, if you use a talisman to acquire wealth, then you will become more dexterous and dynamic, understand what can bring you profit, and avoid unnecessary expenses and risks. In this case, you have everything because of the intuition and new business skills given to you by nature and strengthened by the influence of the talisman. For this kind of talisman, the body parts of various animals whose properties can be transferred to a person are often used. These body parts include the teeth of a shark, a wolf's fang, the claws of tigers or bears, and an eagle's or owl's feathers.

The word *amulet* comes from Latin *amuletum,* which translates as "protective," and is meant to avert sorcery and shield from disease, poison, wounds, and other calamities. An amulet is an object that gives protection. There's also the theory that the Arabic *hamala* (translated as "carry") became the basis for this term. As a rule, amulets are worn hung around the neck. Most ancient amulets involve an image of totemic creatures, sacred animals, and human body parts. These include an Egyptian scarab beetle, an all-seeing eye, a splayed hand, and so forth.

The main influence of an amulet is based on external influence; that is, on external protection and acquisition of the blessings and goods from the world surrounding you. In this case, everything happens not because of your personal abilities and skills but thanks to secret movements in the common astral space due to the work of external forces. If you use an amulet instead of a talisman to acquire wealth, then your desires will be fulfilled at the expense of the space surrounding you. Money can come to you by itself, without your active participation. At the same time, however, if you do not have the professional qualities and skills of handling money, you can easily lose all that you have gained. Often the difference between a talisman and an amulet is rather arbitrary.

The fact is that it is impossible to treat a person as an isolated object. Any inner change that you make leads to a change in the external world, and vice versa—the world around you will change you. Therefore, using something as a talisman will eventually give you what the amulet has to offer. The development of your inner qualities will bring the movement of external forces, and changing external movements will give a new personal stimulus. That is why, in many cases, the words *talisman* and *amulet* are considered synonyms.

Finally, there are natural and man-made talismans and amulets. The natural ones are objects that already have a considerable magical power as part of their nature. That power is suitable for a particular situation or a specific case and doesn't need any special additional actions for it to be effective. These include stones, minerals, metals, herbs, sacred relics, and things found in sacred areas: gold, silver, diamonds, rubies, stones with holes or unusual natural patterns, fossils, sea shells, mandrake root, holy water, and so on.

Man-made talismans and amulets are objects that have undergone certain transformations through a magic ritual, the use of magic spells, or the application of secret symbols. An object that is chosen as an amulet or a talisman is infused with magical power, as a result of which its own natural properties are amplified, or it's assigned a new functional meaning, a new value and effect. These are no longer objects of the physical world but instead magical devices able to transform time and space and change the fates of other things and objects that appear in its sphere of influence. Graphic talismans have a distinct place among man-made objects with magical influence, so we'll talk about them in a different section.

SECRET SIGNS AND MAGIC SYMBOLS

The parallel astral world is inaccessible in conventional understanding. The language of spirits and angels cannot be recorded in simple words. The world of shadows communicates with us through images and signs that emerge in our subconscious. In other words, the astral world tries to communicate in our language to help us understand. And for our words to be accessible to parallel space, we must use the symbols known to it.

All these symbols and signs are like the names of those forces necessary to attain your aspirations and desires. When these "names" are united by one goal and are in constant tension, they become not only "written" but also very real actions. The forces behind these names create conditions and situations that are capable of changing our world. But for changes to really begin happening in our lives, it's not enough to just paint secret signs on a sheet of paper. These symbols must represent your words and actions and become the vessels of your energy and desire. Reading them should make you not only move your lips but also should set in motion the hidden laws of the universe.

SOURCES OF MAGICAL POWER

For a sorcerer or sorceress* to practice magic, power is necessary, but where can one get it? There are born sorcerers, people with superabilities and spiritual people who have direct contact with the Higher Powers. They, frankly speaking, do not need rituals. They have a direct connection to the Source, to the energy flow. However, most sorcerers are people of the soul who subtly feel energies but who do not have an inborn knowledge of magic. The key, a connection with the Higher Powers, can be obtained through initiation from a master or through rituals and places of power. In the Russian tradition of magic, there are six main places of power. They are ancient ruins, burial grounds (cemeteries), nature, the sun, the black sun, and the church.

Ancient ruins: These can be ancient burial mounds, ancient settlements, ruins, shrines, or pagan stones that are traces of ancient cults, rites, and

---

*There are major differences between males and females in the practice of witchcraft, but these differences are beyond the scope of this book. In this book, we are focusing on the aspects of witchcraft that can generally be practiced by both sorcerers and sorceresses.

remnants of the energy of ancient religions. When using these places for magic, it should be remembered that one can enter into a strong internal conflict with one's own worldview and beliefs if one is internally alien to the old traditions of a specific religious site.

Burial grounds (cemeteries): Since the time of Christianization, a powerful *egregore,* or collective mind, was created by hundreds of years of lamenting for the deceased. The essence of the cemetery comes from the energy that people bring there, and not from summoning the dead as many believe. People create powerful energy vortices over burial places (which, by the way, is very dangerous and exhausting for a sorcerer but extremely effective for a magical ritual). As with ancient ruins, remember that when using these sites for magic, you can encounter a strong conflict between ideologies if you are internally alien to the old traditions embodied by the site.

Nature: Natural places such as a forest, mountain, steppe, river, swamp, and other places where a person can find refuge from the city and from society are also power sources. These places harbor deep hidden opportunities that begin to appear due to a shift in your environment and making a change. It is good to go to the mountains alone for four days and to sleep under the stars without a tent. The first day, your mind is swarmed with an endless inner dialogue, but later it stops and is replaced by the state that comes when you find the animus, or the inner Self, of a sorcerer.

The sun: The sun is the only real visible undeniable god. Without the sun, life ends. The sun is the source of life. The sun is an equivalent of a folk god, to whom the so-called Christians appeal in countless spells. He's an analogue to the day, the White God, or Christ.

The black sun: The black sun, black god, Satan, devil, and night are the other side of the coin. By meditating, specifically by connecting to the White God of the sun or the Black God of the sun, you are filled up with energies of creation or destruction, depending on the task you have set out to do. Remember that evil is occasionally good, and the sun often ruins crops. God and the devil are two sides of the same coin and are together parts of the true, complete God.

The church: The sixth place is church. The church is the most common temple type in Russia and therefore has been used in magic since ancient times. The very structure and shape of churches with their domes make them wonderful energy hubs. Remember that people often experience feelings of grace during a divine service, such as during a vigil service or on the days of the Twelve Great Feasts. This is the manifestation of the resonating properties of the dome. Human energy is reflected by the arch, and though it is supposedly directed at God, it returns to those who pray, giving them a feeling of bliss. This is the energy used in all sorts of church sorcery.

❋

A sorcerer who performs a ritual while focusing on a goal in a place of power creates the necessary connection between the sorcerer and God; in this way the sorcerer more accurately transforms himself or herself into God at the time of the rite.

WHO ARE THE SORCERESSES IN RUSSIA?

A common, earthly person, who lives day-by-day and has a narrowed consciousness, is burdened by piled-up, everyday problems and is unable to perform all the necessary magical actions alone. It's very difficult to learn spells by heart, have sleepless nights, collect herbs, and constantly be in the process of self-education. Such people are better off seeking help from professionals rather than tempting fate with independent attempts at performing magical actions.

Since ancient times, people with spell-casting abilities have been feared and respected at the same time. Previously it was believed that sorceresses were lonesome women, leading secluded and solitary lifestyles. Most often they settled on the outskirts of villages or in deep forests, where it was possible to perform sorcery without attracting the attention of others. They collected various berries, rootlets, herbs, and plants and performed magic.

The magic they used could be either dark or white. In ancient times, the label of "sorceress" wasn't limited to evil witches but was also given to herbalists, healers, and botanists who practiced only white magic. Most of the spells used by such women have survived to this day.

In Russia, there have been a lot of sorceresses since those ancient times. They all used different forms of sorcery for their practices. One of the most dangerous forms was taking trail dirt from under a person's feet and throwing it into the wind. What was this sorcery? A sorceress would take the dirt from the footstep of a person she wanted to ruin. She put that dirt on her palm and uttered a curse. Then she walked past the house of her intended victim and blew that spelled dirt over the threshold or gate. Afterward, that person's death was inevitable.

So, how does someone become a sorceress? Sorceresses are most often girls who from the moment of their birth receive magical powers. They have this power even if they do not perform special rituals or cast spells to feel the flow of magical energy. In addition, a sorceress can inherit a gift for magic from another sorceress. It is common knowledge that a dying sorceress must pass on her power. Usually sorceresses can foresee their death two or three days in advance, and during this time they can prepare to transfer the heritage. But if a sorceress cannot make those preparations, she realizes that the evil spirits will not let her go and will begin to torment her. Therefore, when in great agony, sorceresses will often throw off their power onto any random person. If that person receives the sorceress's power without knowing, they will be unable to cope with it, and it will cause great pain.

Magical powers can also be transferred by a mutual agreement. This method is called the "song of the sorceress." Depending on the state of a sorceress's health, the song can last for several nights. The sorceress begins the monologue at midnight and stops talking when roosters begin to crow in the morning, then continues the next night. The successor does not have the right to record or write down any information he or she receives and so must memorize everything. To facilitate the process, elder sorceresses in ancient times often passed on knowledge in the form of a story. This is why people started referring to this as "the song of the sorceress."

There's one more way to become a sorceress, which is to learn sor-

Fig. 2.1. A witch performs a treatment on a patient who is showing symptoms of schizophrenia and acting violently. The witch works to "cool down" the patient. Photograph from 1914.

cery yourself. Sorcerers believe that anyone, young or old, if willing, can become a sorcerer. To do this, one needs to learn the rules of magic, believe in one's own power, and most importantly, conduct a special sorceress's rite and read the spells of powerful sorceresses.

Magic played an important role in the lives of Eastern Slavs, especially peasants. It was impossible to do anything without it. It was widely used in medicine, as sorceresses used spells and charms, often combined with worldly practices, as well as medicinal plants or psychotherapy. Water, fire, and eggs were highly esteemed by the Russian sorceresses.

Magic was also an important part of calendar rituals related to the household, agriculture, sowing, harvesting, moving livestock to pastures, and family life, birth, marriage, and death. Rituals often included acts such as submerging something in water, jumping over fire, and using fur coats to symbolize wealth.

The most common form of mind-driven magic was sorcery. Sorceresses were considered capable of depriving the cow of milk, spoiling crops, and causing illness and even death to individuals, as well as charming young people, protecting people from disease, and defending against the incantations of other sorceresses.

Magic is closely related to religion. In the Middle Ages, the white magic that was widely used in Eastern Europe (Ukraine, Russia) invoked saints and angels, and the dark magic appealed to "unclean spirits" such as devils and demons.

All that I am describing is usually explained away as figments of imagination, inventions of sick minds, or fairy tales for children in our pragmatic, computerized world, but there are things that you can't avoid seeing and noticing. It is still very difficult to explain these things from a scientific point of view. For example, there are people who, at first glance, are not different from those around them, but they know what will happen to this or that person in the future. There are people who can cast a spell on others, can make one person fall in love with another, who can heal without medication. Of course, I'm talking about sorceresses. Some of the sorceresses used to be called Baba Yaga, but a Baba Yaga is not an ordinary sorceress. She is an elder sorceress with great experience in the art of sorcery.

FOLKLORE ABOUT SORCERY

Faith in sorcerers and sorceresses comes from the days of yore and is widely present in Russian villages and cities to this day. Sorcerers and sorceresses were labeled as people in possession of magical knowledge who used it mainly for bad purposes, to harm others. It was believed that they had connections to evil spirits, that they sold their soul to the devil. There is a legend that says that sorcerers and sorceresses first appeared in Kiev and then scattered across the land. Local names of sorcerers and sorceresses indicate their possession of special knowledge, the scope and nature of their activities, and their methods of sorcery. So words like *witch doctor* (ведьмак), *warlock* (ведун), and *witch* (ведьма) were derived from the verb for "to manage" (ведать) and the meaning of "to know" (знать).

People believed that individuals engaged in practices of magic were usually elderly, bereaved, foreign, and unwed. However, there are mythological stories about sorcerers who were young and also those who had families. A sorcerer's nature could be inherited at birth or acquired at a certain age, whether voluntarily or by force. According to some beliefs, children born of a woman and a devil, cursed by their mothers in the womb, or who are illegitimate and born in the third generation of extramarital children would become sorceresses. The latter ones, according to popular belief, were born with tails. From the moment of birth, a sorcerer could be a so-called two-toothed child. This meant that a child was born with two erupting teeth or with two rows of teeth. In North Russian spells, the caster often asks for protection from the two-toothed. An ordinary woman could become a sorceress if she let the devil or the soul of a deceased person possess her, if she cohabited with the devil, or if she made a deal with him.

Magical powers and sorcery abilities could be inherited from a mother or a grandmother who was a sorceress or from a dying sorcerer or sorceress. Numerous mythological stories indicate that any person could receive supernatural power by making a contract with an evil spirit. To become a sorcerer, it was necessary to hold a special ritual of consecration, in which magical power and help were acquired. Usually such rituals were performed in "unclean" places; for example, in a bathhouse, at a crossroads, or in a forest. According to popular beliefs, the one to become a sorcerer made a contract directly with an evil spirit. In the tales of common folk, the one who wanted to know the secrets of sorcery had to go to the crossroads at the crack of dawn for several days. Sometimes, when signing a contract, an elder sorcerer would be present. There they must invoke Satan and take off their cross; then renounce Christ, kin, earth, sun, moon, stars; and then ask the devils to help them learn sorcery. There he would seal his request with blood that he put on his head, so that Satan would hear his plea. In some areas, it was believed that a man, before becoming a sorcerer, brought to the unclean spirits at crossroads an offering, such as a stolen rooster, a sheep, or the bones of dead relatives. Then he was offered a test to curse one member of his household, and only then would he sign a blood contract with an unclean force.

Not every man could cope with the tests put before him, and he would become a victim of unclean forces. If the test was passed, the impure force gave the newly made sorcerer helpers for his whole life. He was obliged to provide these helpers with work. But after his death, the sorcerer would be at the disposal of evil spirits. In popular belief, only an adult who was full of strength could become a sorcerer. There was not enough vitality and intellect in ordinary children or adolescents for this occupation; they were not able to deal with a sorcerer's powers or the aid from unclean spirits. The peasants believed that the transfer of magical power to a child would inevitably lead to death, since the demons that are usually in the service of sorcerers torture and tear apart a weak host. In addition, people were deeply convinced that children could not contain evil, and unclean forces could not destroy the soul of an innocent child.

According to folk descriptions, sorcerers are distinguished by an unusual appearance among ordinary people, including traits inherent in demonic creatures. When discussing the appearances of sorcerers and sorceresses, Russian peasants pay attention primarily to their teeth, hair, eyes, and sight. The appearances of these individuals in villages are significant and unusual. Sorcerers were mostly old people, with long gray hair and beards and long uncut nails. They often have iron teeth, skin darker than that of a Gypsy, and terrifying eyes. In legends, sorcerers are "hollow-eyed," as their eyes do not show reflections of other people. In some places, it is said that if a person looks a sorcerer or a sorceress in the eye, he is reflected upside down in their pupils. A sorcerer never looks directly at his conversational partner, and thick intertwined eyebrows hang over his eyes. The hair of sorcerers is often black, red, or gray.

The Vologda peasants believed that a sorcerer's eyes had no lashes and glowed like burning fire. He had two long teeth, similar to fangs, long fingers, and curved legs. In the Vyatka province, sorcerers were said to have constantly messy hair, excellent beards, and wild eyes with the whites turned outward. Sorcerers and sorceresses were often portrayed with physical disabilities, such as a hump, a stoop, a limp, blindness, or the loss of an eye. In addition, Russians everywhere believed that sorceresses had a tail, and peasants of the South Russian provinces, like Ukrainians, believed the same was true of sorcerers. Sorcerers were connected to anthropomorphic mythological beings and natural spirits not only by many of their external features, including stiffness, sharp and large teeth, and flaming eyes, and so on, but also by some behavioral characteristics.

They, like members of the lower demonology, do not like to show themselves by day and dislike being disturbed by anyone. Sorcerers are often said to be sullen, silent, unsociable, and easily offended. On the other hand, sorceresses are sometimes credited with immeasurable talkativeness. Such people are constantly asking people for something, and you need to be careful with them, as you can give away your fortune to said sorceress with any objects that you give.

Although there were commonly held beliefs as to what were quite clear identifying marks for sorcerers and sorceresses, peasants often noted that it was difficult to recognize them just by their appearance. They would try to behave like fellow villagers so as not to give themselves away. For example, they would confess and take communion to divert suspicion. Sorcerers were often seen as the most pious in the church. They stood close to the icons, bowed to the ground, and liked to light candles near the icons. However, their candles would burn poorly and often fell.

The Russians had the notion that during Christmas or Easter service you can recognize a sorceress in the church by the fact that she is standing with her back to the altar, holding a pail on her head, trying to touch the icons or the priest's robes, or not wanting to leave the church with the procession.

The magical abilities of sorcerers and sorceresses were great. They had the ability to fly, turn into animals and inanimate objects, and also transform other people. When casting curses and sending diseases to this or that victim, person or animal, they used ordinary household items that have striking properties, such as needles, pins, knives, and so on. As a substitute for the victim they would use clothes, dishes, a piece of clothing, hair, nails, fur, and the ground from under the victim's feet or hooves. But the main instruments of sorcery, as well as healing, were spell words. Mythological stories about the conversion of an entire wedding party into wolves or bears by sorceresses were widespread in Russia. Usually, peasants say that curses come on the wind. They then appear in the form of a disease, from which this or that person begins to suffer. In such cases, they turned to healers or sorcerers for help. When expelling the curse, healers would return it to the original sender. Such a turn of events could lead to hostility and confrontation between sorcerers. This usually ended with the death of one of them.

Placing a curse on a man could end not only with him contracting a severe illness or developing a lifelong disability but also with sending him to the grave. Along with the dangerous impact on people, the main harmful actions that sorcerers and sorceresses performed involved ruining crops and livestock and taking away a cow's milk. For peasants these were all considered great sins. Peasants tried to make sure that a sorceress couldn't milk a cow for the first time after it gave birth, as they believed that she would then milk the cow for a whole year. A witch would steal milk mostly at night, and especially on the morning before the holiday of Ivan Kupala. She would go to the field where the cows were early in the morning and call to her those whose milk she wanted, while scraping dew from the grass with her hands. The malicious actions sorcerers practiced on people were not limited to invoking illnesses and upsetting weddings. Sorcerers could make people quarrel, jinx their career, forcibly enchant them, and incite one person to love another and vice versa. They could exhaust lovers or spouses.

Often wizards took revenge for insults, bad food, or lack of rever-

Fig. 2.2. Healer (witch) performs a cleansing rite with blessed water to remove a curse from a child. Photograph from 1914.

ence, especially during a wedding. Women who were natural sorceresses often settled scores with their fiancés. If they cheated or wouldn't marry them, or if a sorceress was dying and her fiancé remained alive, she'd try to drag him with her to the next world.

To carry out their malicious acts and frighten ordinary people, sorcerers and sorceresses often took on the appearance of animals or inanimate objects. Most often they turned into birds, such as magpies and crows. They also turned into wolves, cats, dogs, pigs, and other creatures. Frequently they turned into objects such as moving wheels, stacks or bundles of hay, balls of yarn, sieves, and so forth. According to popular belief, a sorceress in the guise of a pig could break through any lock and could only be driven away by an aspen stake. She liked to wait for a person in that form and then ride him all night until the first rooster's crow. Sorcerers and sorceresses could turn ordinary people into animals that could be dangerous to fellow villagers. It was only possible to neutralize or kill such shape-shifters with one backhand stroke, as well as the sorcerers themselves, in the traditional view.

People were convinced that a sorcerer, like a sorceress, could not die until his knowledge passed to another person. A sorcerer could pass his ability to perform magic once in life, either in full or partially, and as a rule, just before his death. Magical knowledge is inherited, and if there was no successor, then he would pass it to anyone willing. Even if there was no one who wanted it, the sorcerer would try to transfer his skills to any person, even with trickery. For example, he might try to transfer it by direct contact with them or by handing them any object. As he made the transfer, the sorcerer would say the words, "To you!" Sometimes the stories of peasants tell us that it is possible to transfer knowledge to an inanimate object, like a stick, and throw it in the road. Whoever lifts the object will receive the sorcerer's powers.

In some mythological stories, a desperate, dying sorcerer will use the inexperience of a child who takes a mug of water or something else from him at his request. One of the stories tells about a boy who took a mug from a sorcerer and later began to hear voices: "Give us work, give us work!" And soon the boy died because he was unable to cope with the power that was transferred to him.

Common knowledge says that a long and difficult death is sent to sorcerers and sorceresses as punishment for their sins. Peasants believed that terrible torments awaited such sinners in the afterlife. The death of a sorcerer produced an adverse effect even on nature. Strong winds would rise as he suffered. There was a belief that sorcerers who died before the contract that they signed with an unclean force expired didn't lose their strength after death. Instead, they continued to harm people. In addition, sorcerers, just like terrible sinners and apostates, were not accepted by the earth and would continue to roam around after death.

The burial of a sorcerer was different from that of a normal person. If the sorcerer didn't die at home, he was not brought into the house and was buried instead at the place of his death. If he died at home, he was taken out of the hut headfirst, not feetfirst like an ordinary person. Much of what people did during a sorcerer's funeral was intended to ensure that he couldn't find his way back and disturb people even after death. Thus, while he was carried toward the grave, his coffin would be turned around several times, first with his feet forward, then with his head. Before the procession reached the cemetery, it would stop and turn the deceased sorcerer face down. The tendons in his legs were cut so that he couldn't walk away from his burial place after death. In Saratov province, for the same purpose, a deceased sorceress's heels were cut and then stuffed with hog hair.

Russians and other Eastern Slavs in almost every region believed that the thing that would save them from the unrest of the walking dead sorcerer was the piercing of his grave and coffin by an aspen stake. In some places, to stop a dead sorcerer from roaming the earth, an aspen board was embedded in the bottom of his coffin, aspen shavings were laid in it, and aspen branches were placed in the form of a cross at the bottom.

The burial places of sorcerers and sorceresses were considered dangerous and scary. People tried to avoid them, but in areas where droughts often occurred, peasants were forced to perform special rites at the graves of sorcerers. They believed that droughts and, accordingly, bad harvests were sent to the villagers by the "unclean" dead, including dead sorcerers. Therefore, to bring rain, old women would go to the grave of a sorcerer at night and pour water on it to "wash away the deceased."

The Spells

A spell is not just used to affect another person. It is the creation of a common new world with room for two. A love spell can be not only a curse—the process of enslavement, attaching yourself to a person by invoking their passion against their will—but also can be a process of building and creation. It's up to you to choose what suits you better. And in general your choice will be based on your own religious beliefs.

A FEW WORDS ABOUT SPELLS

The subject of the spell needs to be weaker than you. This is a necessary truth. You must not cast a spell by yourself on someone who is energetically stronger than you. In that case, you need the help of other people or a sorcerer. A sorcerer is generally a conductor of energy, not the source. However, that isn't always the case.

Magic is an interaction at the energy level, and the spell ritual is only a link between you and the object of your passion.

If you cannot collect the amount of magical power or energy necessary to perform the rite on your own, then you can connect to an outer egregor, the church, the forces of nature, or some other place of power.

The world is a multifaceted whole system in which the particles of the whole (including us) interact with each other, directly or indirectly. By performing a magical rite, an action, we set in motion a cause-and-effect liaison that is likely to lead you to the achievement of your goal. However, you will lose something, and there will be a rearrangement of your life.

On the other hand, we can assume that the fact that you are casting a binding spell or performing some magical action means that this is *already* embedded in the program of your life. The world is a rigid structure, where the chain of relationships is the framework on which human life is built. But karma or fate is but a piece of a human's life, and the higher a person ascends on a ladder of knowledge, magic, and one's own path, the more the range of possibilities will expand, and the corridor—the range of one's perception of reality—will widen.

THE LANGUAGE OF SPELLS

The use of words as a magic spell (incantation) is a concept familiar to us from childhood. A spell is a sequence of words with a certain rhythm and order that gives them a particular sound, made to achieve any purpose. A sorcerer uses a spell to accomplish the desired effect. It doesn't matter what language the words are in, as this does not diminish the effectiveness of the action, and in some cases even increases it. The spell is usually composed in a poetic format. Spells come in different styles and sizes, but their crucial feature is the rhythm used to say them. This rhythm helps a sorcerer enter into a kind of trance and complete the planned rite. Spells can apply to various spheres: love, finances, influencing a person or nature, or addressing the dweller of another world. Along with spells, more experienced sorcerers often use additional auxiliary materials such as plants, stones, knives, candles, and much more.

THE POWER BEHIND SPELLS

The working mechanism of a spell is very intriguing and causes superstitious fear among people uneducated on the topic. Judge for yourself. The practitioner makes the necessary preparations and begins to read the spell that collects the force from the surrounding space, gently pulling it together and twisting it around himself. It appears as a powerful cyclone, spinning with tremendous force. This is the energy used by the sorcerer to realize his intentions. The vibrations that occur when saying words with a certain rhythm and directed intention can perform genuine miracles. The areas in which people use spells are very different, from household magic to healing.

As you read a spell, the algorithm of magic acts in the most direct way, affecting nature and people. Ancient spells work regardless of whether you believe in them. Words that are part of a spell can often be incomprehensible to a modern person, but they shouldn't be replaced, as the result of your work depends on it.

Spells range from very simple (whispers) to quite elaborate and difficult to pronounce, such as the ones meant for solving fairly complex problems. You can charm water for health, and it will take minimal time and energy, but you cannot just say the text aloud with an image in your mind and expect an instant change from negative to positive. You will need a whole set of measures and a built-in work pattern, even for a spell that seems simple on the surface.

The spell needs to be read and spoken from the heart, melodiously, aloud or in a low voice, with mental focus on the result. As you work with spells, you must demonstrate your sincerity and faith. You should have no doubts about what you do; you haven't resorted to such means for help lightly. You must know that it will work and affect your situation as you want it to.

The following chapters offer spells about various aspects of human life: love and relationships; money, wealth, and business; protection; house and home; health and healing; and dreams and divination. In some cases, a spell could easily fall into more than one category, but to avoid repetition, I have just classified each by its dominant theme.

These spells can be used on any gender; we adapt spells based on the current situation. Blanks have been left in the spells for you to fill in your own name and any other names that particular spell might require. A sorcerer performing these spells for someone else would fill in the names of the people for whom he is performing the work.

3

Love and Relationship Spells

God created the first humans as androgynous, universal, and ideally happy creatures containing both sexes, but later still divided them into two halves—and this is where we get men and women. And since then, to gain lost happiness and integrity of being, these two halves of one whole are looking for each other. And in the whole, vast, sublunar world there is only one half who is the other half of you. Finding this other half is the goal of life for everyone.

The desire to love and be loved and to be with your beloved one is the natural desire of every human being. Sometimes relationships between two halves are not always perfect: either a rival turns out to be more grasping or beautiful and takes your love away or takes a loving husband and father from his family, or the fire between a couple goes out and there is no passion left after years of marriage.

A love spell is the binding to you of a person who is the object of your passion or unrequited love, through various magical actions. It helps you to set the fire of passion and desire into your relationship and to restore lost love.

PLATONIC LOVE AND RESPECT SPELLS

❋ Spell to Be Loved and Respected

To receive love and respect from others, get up early, even before the roosters, go to an open field and, as soon as the sun rises, cross your arms over your chest and read the following charm:

> *I got up in the morning, went out into an open field, looked in all four directions and at the red sun. As all honest people look at and desire the red sun, so will everyone look at and desire me. Everyone, from all the old men and women to all the young guys and beautiful girls. My words are the key to the lock from now until forever.*

With the last words of the charm, extend your arms forward sharply, then spread them apart. Stay that way for a while, holding your hands out in front of you, then go home.

❋ Praise Spell to Be Done in July

On the nights of July 7, 9, and 12, gather dew in three different vessels. Pour three drops of dew out of each vessel and say:

> *I'll bathe in bright dew, in maidenly beauty. I will surround myself with the bright stars; I will gird myself with the silver moon. For today, for the whole year, I will shine whiter than the light of the full moon, will be more beautiful than the red sun for all those who live here and all those who do not. Let them all notice me, let all the doors in front of me open, let everything I say and everything I do be praised.*

❋ Peacock Talisman

Anyone who has a peacock's feather as a talisman will always be a favorite of society. You do not need to carry a whole feather; it is enough to have only the upper part, the plume. You can also use jewelry, brooches, and earrings in colors and shapes reminiscent of this graceful bird's feathers.

❈ Oak Leaf Spell

To become well known and gain popularity, coat one side of an oak leaf with fresh honey. Stick this leaf to the west wall on the outside of your house and say:

> *As this leaf sticks to my wall, so will prosperity and a good reputation stick to me, forever and ever.*

❈ Spell to Change Attitudes

Everyone needs love, but not everyone can feel it. In addition to romantic feelings, some suffer from the anger and negativity of those around them, and so there is an irresistible desire to change everything, to prove that you are worthy of respect. This can be achieved through this charm. But first of all, you must change your attitude toward yourself and become a confident, strong person. When uttering the following magical words, invest all your kindness and faith for the better:

> *I turn to all the saints: as you help the suffering, so bless me too, [name]. The blue sea rose, the waves rose to the skies, the sky became troubled and burst with thunder and lightning. So the people surrounding me erupt in their anger, but I'll get up, cross myself, I'll go to the icon, I'll pray, I'll ask for love, I will save my soul from suffering, and whoever looks at me will immediately see all the bright and good that is in my heart. No more will people speak evil to me or send misfortune my way. Those who speak with me will be filled with respect toward me. My heart is open, so let others be kind to me. In the name of the Father and the Son and the Holy Spirit. Amen.*

Repeat the charm as necessary for several days. Very soon you will notice that other people's attitudes toward you have changed for the better.

SPELLS TO FIND A LOVED ONE AND REMOVE LOVE CURSES

❈ Charm on a Loved One

If you cannot unite with your one and only in any way, this charm will help you find your loved one. You must conduct a special ceremony. You must go out of town, into nature, to a village where there is a river. As the moon appears in the sky, go to the shore, walk around, and weave a wreath of herbs and twigs. Then read any prayer you know over the wreath. Go down to the river, step ankle deep into the water, then put your wreath into the water and say the following charm to find a loved one three times:

> *Swim, my joy, through pure water to the one who will bring warmth to my soul and light the hearth in my house.*

Then cross yourself and read the prayer again. You will soon see that your personal life will change very quickly.

❋ Find a New Love

If your lover left you, and you think that the best remedy to mend your broken heart will be a new love, do the following: Set on the table a large porcelain cup or bowl, a large mirror, and a pink candle. Sit at the table and light the candle. Throw dry leaves of strawberries, red rose petals, and melissa grass into the bowl. Add to them three drops of lavender or rue oil. Stir all herbs in the bowl with your hands. Doing this, gaze into the depth of the mirror and say:

These herbs together are brought
To seek new love I have in mind
New passion I seek to attract
Peace and happiness I aim to find.

Fold the herbal mixture into a pink pouch. Place it next to an amethyst crystal and white dove's feather. Always carry this amulet with you, until you meet your new love.

❋ How to Remove a Curse of Solitude

If several generations of women in your family have had problems with their personal life, there may be a feeling of the effects of a wreath of celibacy or curse of solitude. This should be diagnosed by an experienced sorcerer. If you are a practitioner yourself, use the following rite of solitude. Take eggs from a village, not a store. You will need seven eggs. Read any prayer you know over them. Break one egg into a glass of water and put it at the head of your bed at night. You must also read the following charm over it to remove the curse of solitude:

By the strength of an egg and the power of an elegant phrase, remove the curse from my face, from my hands, from my feet, and from my body. As life force is born in the egg, so a new power is born in me, and the curse dies away. So shall it be.

In the morning, pour the egg and water into a container and put it in a cold place. Repeat the ceremony for seven days in a row. Take the container with all the yolks and water out into nature and bury it while saying:

Mother Earth, take this curse away from me.

❊ Charm for Beauty and Attractiveness

If you are categorically unlucky in your personal life, you do not have a loved one, and you think that you do not have enough charm, this charm will help with beauty and attractiveness. Take a ripe apple and read these words over it:

As this fruit has been attracting others from the beginning of time, so my companion will be conquered. Amen.

Afterward, cut the apple into two halves, eat one half, and leave the other at a crowded crossroad.

❊ Prayer against Loneliness

If you still have not found happiness in your personal life and have neither family nor a loved one, this prayer against loneliness will help. You must go to the forest, find three anthills, and read this prayer against loneliness over each one:

There is no evil without good, no wealth without labor, no faith without a cross. So I, by the will of Christ, will not be lonely. In the name of the Father and the Son and the Holy Spirit.

After reading the prayer, leave something sweet on each anthill.

❊ Prayer to Be Married

If you are alone, but you want to be married, have a family, love, and be loved, this rite for marriage will help. You must perform the ritual at midnight during the first quarter of the moon. Go out into your yard or where no strangers may be. Wear new, white clothes without embroideries or ornaments. Touch your heart with your left hand, lift your right hand to the sky, and say:

As the moon is hidden, so it will be full and clear.
My half is hidden in darkness, it is not open to me.
As days go by, lead a dear friend to me, so that we can become one whole,
Under the full moon, and in the light of day.
I'm waiting for you, my betrothed, and there is a place ready for you.
I, [name] am the heavenly bride sent to you. Amen.

Go home and sleep on new white bed linens, without images or designs. If a man becomes acquainted with you before the full moon comes, he is sent to you from above. If not, repeat the ceremony next month.

❊ How to Remove the Wreath of Celibacy

The wreath of celibacy is nothing but a curse transmitted by genes. The mistakes of previous generations—your mom, grandmother, and great-grandmother—are the root of the wreath of celibacy. Since the full genetic memory is enclosed in the hair, often hair is used to remove the wreath of celibacy. One way to remove it is to do this: Cut at least 1 inch of hair, put it in a fire-resistant bowl, and burn it with these words:

Memory in the wreath, wreath on my head and in my female genes. I'll burn my hair and put it in the casket, where my loneliness and celibacy belong. I'll bury a casket, and with it the celibacy wreath. So it is.

Put the ash in a tin box and bury it on a riverbank.

SPELLS TO ATTRACT A MATE OR MAKE A FRIEND DESIRE YOU

❊ Make a Friend Desire You

If you really like a man, but he does not notice you in any way, or notices you only as a good friend, you can use this special rite. At night, place a basin of water outside, and in the morning bathe in this water, saying this spell:

> *Like the moon, I am needed; like water, I'm gentle. As the traveler walks through the desert and falls to the water, so the good fellow will come to me kindly, as if he has found water in the desert. Amen.*

Wipe off the water with the hem of your shirt. Repeat the ritual for one lunar month.

❊ Win Your Beloved's Love

To win the love of your chosen one, light a pink or red candle and place on the table a small white handkerchief. Drip melted candle wax on this handkerchief so that a heart-shaped figure forms on the fabric. First, mark the outline of the heart, and then fill the shape with wax. When the wax hardens, write on it the name of your chosen one, and plug a long sharp splinter, or a needle, into this waxy heart. Doing this witchcraft, repeat the spell:

> *Flame is not lit, but soul invoked.*
> *Wax is not spilled, for body is called.*
> *My heart I don't pierce, love is brought forth.*
> *The soul and body will unite,*
> *In the blessed [name] with might,*
> *The heart will be filled with love,*
> *For me, blessed [name] will fall.*

When you have finished this action, hide the heart with the inserted needle in a place where no one will find it. Do not wait for the results of your sorcery; take action on your own. Try to be as close as possible to the one to whom your spells were directed, and in general help him show his feelings to you.

❋ Attract with Flowers

Collect and dry the flowers of a rose or jasmine. If you want to attract the attention of a person you like, put these dried flowers in a small cup, sprinkle them with alcohol, and set them on fire. When the fire burns and the smoke rises from the flowers, whisper on it:

How this smoke burns and melts we see,
Thus heart and soul of God's servant [name] burn for me,
God's servant [name].

❋ Make Your Beloved Desire You

Write on a sheet of paper these words:

Without blessing, I will rise,
Without crossing forward will go,
Out from house, through the door,
Into dark forests and rotten moor.
And in those forests there in black bath,
To woman-procurer will show a path.
At her house—a stove in stone,
In her furnace a brass cup lies.
Within that cup is boiling and boiling,
Burns and burns, dries and dries.
Thus about me [name]'s heart boiled,
The blood burned, body withered by day, and night,
With the old moon, and with the new month
Key to my words, strong as tower,
With strength from the Heavenly power.

Light a candle. Set the paper with the written spell on fire. When the paper is but ashes, rub the ash between your palms and say what was written on the paper.

❋ Turn Your Beloved's Heart to You

Spread a black tablecloth on the table and put a red candle on it. Light the candle. Sprinkle some salt on top of the candle flame and say the spell:

In somber dawn I will rise,
In springwater I won't rinse,
Not in white dew, I'll wipe with sewn cloth,
Not spun, not woven, and not bought,
I'll go out the door, not in the door,
From the cottage, at night through grove
Down the path to a black bath,
In the bathhouse there's a black stove,
In the furnace, the firewood burns.
As [name]'s heart to me, [name] turns
In the day, and at night, and every hour
Key to my words, strong as tower,
With strength from the Heavenly power.

When you have finished reciting the spell, collect all the salt scattered on the tablecloth and spread it in the wind, in a clean field, or sprinkle it at the door of your loved one's house.

❋ Ignite the Feelings of Your Beloved

To ignite feelings in the heart of your chosen one, strike one stone against another stone so that sparks fly, and say the spell:

In the morning I'll go,
Go out to a clean field,
A field where resin pillar stands,
Fiery serpent under it commands.
I bow to that serpent and pray.
Do not burn or scorch me,
But fly to the [name],
Inflame and scorch white body of thee,
Zealous heart, her hot blood,
So that she can't be without me
Nor spend a night, nor dwell by day,
In morning in mind my image stayed,
In evening by bed—to me prayed.
Key to my words, strong as tower,
With strength from the Heavenly power.

⁂ Make Your Beloved Long for You

Near midnight, go to your beloved's house. Grease the front door handle with sunflower oil and speak the following charm:

I will rise at an early dawn,
Wash myself in springwater,
Go out the door and in three doors.
Those doors tightly and firmly close,
Thus tight and firm [name]'s love to me, [name], shows,
In mornings and evenings, days and nights,
Hours and minutes, I'm in her sights,
Can't sleep or lie, about me dreams,
Withers of longing for her dear
Soon the word effect will steer,
Quickly deed is done—we'll hear.

⁂ Bring Tender Feelings to Your Beloved

In order that the beloved begins to experience the same tender feelings that you feel toward him, take advantage of this charm. This rite can be performed with an apple. As has been known for a long time, apples are fruits that have a great and strong energy. So they are able to fulfill any desire, if properly treated.

Take a ripe red apple and cut it vertically and horizontally. The shape of an asterisk should be left in the middle. Between the halves of the apple, put a piece of paper with the name of the one you love written on it. Now take a scarlet thread and tightly bind the fruit. When you do this, read this small magical charm:

Put this delicious apple in the sun, let it grow thirsty day-by-day, and let my beloved, [name], also thirst for me, and as soon as the apple dries up completely, my beloved will come to me and swear his love this day. Let him think of me day and night, let him understand that he cannot live without me, and he will only be happy with me, as I am with him.

After this, set the apple on a windowsill or take it out into the garden in the sun so that it dries out.

❊ Make Your Beloved Pay Attention to You

If you love a man very much, but he does not pay attention to you at all, the following charm will help. Read it over a cup of water:

> *Stormy water, flow into the river; river, flow to the sea. Flow, streams, to a secret place, to the heart of [name]. Let him come to me, open his heart, and cling to me from his soul. Amen.*

Afterward, give the water to the man to drink. You will soon see results.

❊ Enchant Your Beloved with Padlocks

Buy two small padlocks. Use red paint to write the initials of the person you want to enchant on one lock and your initials on the other. When the paint dries, lock the two locks together and close them with the key from his padlock, while saying the following charm:

> *The earth is the sky, the key is the lock, so that he may not escape.*

Afterward, keep the keys from the lock inscribed with your initials. Take the keys to the other lock and throw them in a river or lake (it is important that it is a natural body of water). And as you do so, say the following:

> *I give these keys to the water, I take [name]'s fate into my own hands.*

If you do this ritual correctly and precisely, the person you charm will not be able to go without you for a single day. If later you want to remove this spell—open your lock and throw the lock with his initials into the same river with these words:

> *I give this lock and return [name]'s fate to him. Amen.*

❊ Love Charm with a Special Gift

If you really love a man, but for some reason the two of you are not together, a strong love charm will help you. It will only work when a man is single or divorced. This charm will not work on married men. The family ties will nullify its effect. You must give a special gift to your loved one on his birthday. It must be something original and not ordinary. Special energy channels open on this day. These channels can enhance the effects of a love charm and any other type of charm. Before giving him the gift, read this love charm over it:

> *I will give this gift from my heart and attract the heart not of the one who lies in the ground but of the one who lives above it. Let him not eat or drink until he comes to my home. Key. Lock. My word. Amen.*

You must use this love charm only if you are fully confident of your love for this person.

❈ Remove Your Beloved's Indifference

You unrequitedly fell in love with a man and tried to start a relationship, but it did not lead to anything. He is indifferent to you, and you are crazy with love. In this case, a charm to draw his attention will help. To perform this ritual, you will need any hair accessory: a hair clip, barrette, or elastic band. Every morning, when you braid and style your hair, read the following charm to attract male attention over the chosen accessory:

> *As I'm weaving braids, I'm drawing the attention of [name] to myself. Let him look at me, let him not take his eyes away from me, let him walk around me in circles. Amen.*

Do this for a minimum of fifteen days, and you will see that your chosen one will begin to show interest in you and want to pursue a relationship with you.

❈ Tempt Your Beloved

If you really like a man who does not pay much attention to you or sees you only as a friend, this strong temptation spell will help. For this ritual, you need three kinds of fruit: bananas; peaches or apricots; and apples or figs. You must serve these fruits to your beloved. As you wash the fruit, look at the man and say this love charm:

> *[Name], desire me how I desire you. Take the fruit from my hands; look at me. Do not look away, [name], and know this: my skin is*

> *tender like a peach (apricot), juicy like an apple (fig), sweet like a banana, smooth where it should be, and curvaceous where it should be, for your pleasure. So be it.*

The man must eat the fruit. Repeat the ritual a week later. This man will be yours very soon and will desire you.

❋ Love Spell by the Full Moon

During the full moon, light a pink candle, put three lily blossoms in a glass bowl filled with water, put his photograph on the bottom with your full name written seven times on the back. Inhale the scent of the lilies and read the following charm:

> *On the far shore there is a garden in bloom, where bees fly and pollinate flowers. As the fragrance of flowers attracts these bees, so [name] will be attracted to me, [name]. Let it continue to draw toward me so long as the garden continues to bloom. So shall it be.*

Take the lilies out and dry them in a dark place. Keep them there so long as the charm is working properly.

❋ Awaken Your Beloved's Feelings with a Gift

A spell involving the use of a gift is very strong. Therefore, it is often used when you want to awaken feelings in a person who is completely indifferent to you. This can be because he simply doesn't notice your feelings due to natural inattention. The ceremony is quite simple to perform, since it can be timed to any holiday. It should be remembered that such an effect can only be accomplished if your chosen one is absolutely free and doesn't have serious feelings for another woman.

A charmed thing is given under any pretext that a man would like. It is very important that the thing you use as a gift is appropriate and that he likes it. And it should be remembered that the spell works only if it's performed on a new thing. A used object cannot be used for this gift, even if you are sure that your loved one would find it pleasant.

It is also very important that your gift will be used for a long time. After all, a spell on an object should act on the energy of a loved one for a certain time, so that the initial results will be manifest. And, therefore, the gift item should be used for as long as possible.

Before handing over the acquired gift, you must read this spell:

My dear [name of the chosen one], to you a gift I present,
But in return, peace I take from thee.
You will miss me, and long for me.
Without me you cannot live,
And thus call upon me you shall.
You will come to me and you will love me.

It is very important to remind a sweetheart about you within a few days after gifting by appearing nearby or with a phone call. The result, as a rule, will show very quickly.

❋ Love Charm with Wine

If you fall in love with a man, so much so that your head is spinning, but he perceives you only as a friend, this rite will help you. It is a love charm with wine. On a moonlit night, pour red wine into a decanter and put it on the windowsill. Then you must bend low so that your breath almost touches the surface of the drink, and say the following charm:

Awake, get up, spirits of the vine, from your strong sleep. Gather all your strength and power. Enter [name]'s heart, lead him by his sweet tooth, so that he is drawn to me and looks for me. Make him sweeter than honey.

You must repeat this charm nine times, then knock on the decanter with the heel of your shoe and say:

I'm waiting.

All night, the decanter should stand on the windowsill, moonlighting. When your man comes, you must give him this charmed wine. And very soon this man will be mindlessly in love with you.

❊ Attract Love Using Your Beloved's Property

You can also attract love with the help of an item that your loved one recently touched. You must do it during a full moon. Take any small item that your beloved touched in your hands. It can be anything. At midnight, under a full moon, light a candle. In your left hand, hold your loved one's possession and rub a white feather on it thirty times, moving it clockwise. Take a knife and put it over the flame. When it's hot, use it to break a brown egg, pouring the inside into a glass of holy water. Say:

> *Fly to me, your swan [your name], white-winged [his name]. You do not like to be in the white light without your other half. My word is strong like a stone and deep as the sea.*

Put the item over the glass and cover it with a white cloth. In the morning, take the liquid to his house and pour it into the ground near the wall.

❊ Attract Your Beloved Using an Apple

The Savior of the Apple Feast Day is an Eastern Slavic folk holiday that is observed on August 19. Apples acquire mystical power on this day. At this time of year, this is the easiest way to attract a young man whom you like. On the day when the Apple Savior arrives, go into your garden and choose the most beautiful and ripe apple. Pick it. If you do not have an apple tree, then ask to be allowed to do it at the home of relatives or friends. Do not do this without the knowledge of the owners; you must ask. After picking the apple, give the hostess something in return for the apple, such as spices or jam, not money.

When evening comes, take the fragrant fruit in your hands and stand with it facing the sunset. Imagine the one you love. Divide the apple in two pieces and place a photo of your loved one in the space between the halves. Say his name and this small charm three times:

> *With this fruit you and I will be together forever.*

During the nine days that follow, you should begin the day by placing the fruit in the sun's rays, and in the evening you should place the fruit at the head of your bed. Each time you change the location of the apple, repeat the above ritual, and each time, increase the volume of your voice. If the apple has withered by the ninth day, the ritual went well. If it's rotten, you cannot be together.

SPELLS TO BIND A LOVED ONE

❊ Love Spell with Wine

Purchase a bottle of good red wine at the store. Do not take change. If this is not possible, drop the change at the shop's doorstep. Go home. Close the doors and windows, and make sure that nobody will bother you. Sit in the center of the room and relax. Take the bottle in both hands and hold it up so that while you read the spell your breath touches it. You need to put your maximum of emotions and feelings (energy) into this. Close your eyes, picture before you the image of your beloved, and repeat these words for about ten minutes:

As I speak I spell this wine,
[Name of the chosen one]'s passion to be mine;
His thoughts and feelings, submit to me.
As soon as he sips this wine,
His love eternal will be mine.

Now wrap the bottle in a clean white towel and lay it under your bed. It must stay there for three nights. During this time, the energy of your desire will fully enter the drink. Then within twenty-four hours you need to treat your lover with this wine. To avoid suspicion, think of an occasion in advance.

When the man takes the first sip, inwardly repeat the words of the spell, once is enough, while looking into his eyes.

❊ Love Spell with a Padlock

To spell your chosen one, procure a small padlock. Unlock and hide it under the mat near your door before you invite your lover to visit. After he steps over the threshold, stepping in this way through the lock, and comes into the house, lock the padlock with the key and say:

No one will ever unlock this lock, no one will.
[Name] will not argue with me, or fight, or end.
Key at the bottom, fire in earth, river flows,
By word it is locked, and lock to me goes
Affixed, with a holy spirit christened.

Later, the key should be thrown into a river or a lake, and keep the padlock—hidden and secured.

❋ Bind Your Beloved Using a Birch Twig

Place a birch twig under the threshold of your front door. After your beloved steps over the threshold, move the twig to a dry, hot place and speak three times:

Wither [his name] from love to [your name], wither like this twig is withering.

Repeat these words every day until your spell starts to work, and even after you get what you wanted, do not forget them. Instead of a birch twig in this spell casting, you can use a wheat ear or a birch leaf. The important thing is that they have been picked recently.

❋ Love Charm Using Ripe Beans

To charm a woman you like, take two ripe beans from one pod. When you come to the house of your beloved, hide one of the beans in her bed. Wait for midnight, and knowing that the person you love has already gone to bed, put a second bean into your mouth and say in your mind:

As two beans together grew,
Washed in the same dew,
Fed by the same land,
Enjoyed one and only sun,
Same is now—we should be one,
This one feeling we should share,
Happiness enjoy as a pair.

If you do not have the opportunity to visit said lady's house, carry these two beans with you at all times, and when you meet the one to whom all your feelings and thoughts are directed, silently put one of the beans in her pocket. Put the other bean put in your mouth and say the previous spell in your mind. If even this is not possible for you, bury one bean on a road where your beloved walks every day, and at the moment when she steps over the talisman you made, perform the steps mentioned above.

❊ Charm Using a Two-Colored Apple

You can charm a loved one with the help of an apple. Split an apple that has a bright red side and a green side. Kiss the red half of the apple and say:

One that tastes it—will fall in love.

Then rub the green half of the apple on your chest and say:

One who bites it—will desire.

Give this apple to your chosen one and be sure that they eat the whole apple.

❊ Spell Using Candles and Needles

Before noon, buy two thick candles and eight sharp needles. In the evening, after sunset, use a needle to write the initials of the person you love on the top side of one of the candles. On the other candle, write your own initials in the same way. After that, pin the needles from all sides around the letters, with four needles on each candle. Put the candles one foot apart on a table with no tablecloth and light their wicks. When either of the candles burns down to a needle and the needle falls on the table, blow in the direction in which presumably your favorite is now, and say:

I ask for action, I speak for effect
On the present time I reflect.
Faraway forces I provoke,
Not to stray to the distance invoke,
Not even near, but graft in [name]'s heart,

To yearn for me in his thoughts he'll start,
In his dreams my image will burn
At the evening and dawn, at the morning sun,
By the old moon, and by the new one.

When the last needle drops out of the candles, blow out the flames.

❋ Circle Talisman for Your Chosen One

Cut out two identical paper circles with a diameter of 1.5 inches. A third circle of the same size is to be cut from thin copper sheet or aluminum foil. Write on one of the paper circles your name and date of birth, and on the other write the name and birthday of your chosen one. Use red ink for this. Place all the circles together so that the metal is in the middle and your names are facing it. Pierce a hole through the center of the circles and pass through it a red woolen thread. Tie it with a triple knot, thus securing all three parts of the talisman, and say:

Thus united, together brought,
Soul and body; heart and thought,
Word and deed; fate and life,
A man and a woman, [man's name] and [woman's name],
Once baptized, on [his date of birth] and [her date of birth] born.

Keep this amulet in your house or hide it in the house of your chosen one.

❋ Love Spell with Colored Roses

Take a red and white rose with long stems. Imagine that the white rose is you, and red rose is your chosen one. Weave together the stems of the roses while repeating the spell:

In different colors these roses I find, so I [name] with [name] are two of a kind.
As these flowers together come, so [name] with [name] now will be one.

Tie the ends of the intertwined rose stems at the top and bottom with a red thread so that they don't fall apart, and put them in a crystal vase. Over the next few days, whenever your eyes fall on coupled colors, repeat the spell in your mind, and very soon your words and dreams will become reality. You can use other flowers, but they must have different colors and be the same type of flower.

❋ Bind Your Chosen One at Five O'clock

To bind your chosen one to yourself, at five o'clock in the afternoon, take a scarlet candle in your left hand and well-salted black bread in your right. Stand like that on the front doorstep of your house, face the street, and say:

With bright flames I conjure,
Flesh of the earth I command
In soul and body [name] I demand,
To cling to me by heart and hand
I'll show her kindness, time and again,
On a dark night, and a bright day,
By the new moon and when the old wanes.
For me she withered, but didn't die,
Thinking of me even while dined,
I would be always on her mind.

While saying these words, cross the slice of bread three times. When you have finished your spell, blow out the candle and eat the bread. After that, you shouldn't drink anything until sunset; otherwise the strength of your spell will diminish.

❋ Bind Your Beloved Using Strands of Hair

If you can get three strands of your loved one's hair, add five strands of your own hair to them and throw them together into the fire. While doing this, say:

By fire crowned, never unbound.

If you can get his blood (fresh or dried), dissolve it with alcohol (ethanol) and then pour this alcohol onto a small plate and set it on fire. Hold your left palm directly above the flame and imagine how your chosen's heart begins to burn with love and passion. At this moment, say these secret words:

> *Blood of life, life of love, heat of the flame, flame of lit hearts. With fire bound, will never split, it will not melt, nor fail, so be it!*

❊ Binding with a Ring

If you decide to give a beloved woman a ring, then first perform the following sorcery. Take three strands of your hair and tie them around the ring. Binding the first hair, say:

> *The one, who will wear it, will bind with me in thought and heart.*

With the second strand:

> *The one, who will wear it, will be bound to me with body and soul.*

And with the third strand:

> *The one, who will wear it, will not forget me, will not stop loving me, will not lie to me, and will not go to another.*

Keep this ring until the auspicious day, and when it's time to give it, remove the strands of your hair and give it to your beloved. Hide these hair strands, and while they are intact and secure, your lady will not leave you.

SPELLS TO NOT PART WITH YOUR BELOVED

❊ Spell with Incense Smoke

So as to not part with your loved one, read this spell on the smoke of incense:

> *To rise before sunrise I'll bother,*
> *Wash myself with well water,*
> *I will go to a clean field besides,*
> *Broad and expanding, to the east side*
> *From the east side hut is not shut*

There's a stove, inside that hut
On the stove is a board, on the board longing
I'll raise the board; take longing along,
Put it in the heart, [name]'s very soul.
That he would long for me alone,
This yearning food will not appease,
Nor with the drinks, in mind he sees me,
Key and lock my words will spell.
The lock is locked, key's lost as well.

If you do not have incense, light and then blow out an ordinary candle and say the words into its smoke.

❋ Spell to Not Part with Your Chosen One

So as to not part with your chosen one, write this spell on a sheet of paper:

Before the sun I will rise, and wash at the well,
Go from door to door, from gate to gate,
Into a clear field, freedom in meadow dwells,
Into the east side I'll gaze.
In eastern side three stoves are there:
From copper, iron, and brick are made
And how those three stoves burn forth
Melt from heaven to earth, south to north
Thus the heart inflamed and blazed is
Body and soul, [name] for me, [your name], feels.
And from copper my words are thicker
Stronger than iron and harder than brick.

Fold this paper into a tube and put a dry wormwood herb in it. Then set fire to this tube from one end, and say the spell written on it into the smoke.

SPELLS TO MAKE YOUR BELOVED RETURN TO YOU

❋ Spell for Your Beloved to Come Back to You

If you want a beloved person to come back to you, light an orange candle and place it in front of his photograph, or just a paper with his full name written on it. Place on the photograph a glass filled to one-quarter with pure springwater (well water). Throw three pinches of sugar in the water and say:

> *Spirits of Light and Darkness I summon, and spell I devise, (full name of the person) to come when all water dries.*

After completing that, blow out the candle and move the glass and the photograph to a dry, warm place. When all the water from the glass evaporates, the person you desire will come to you.

❋ Spell for Your Lost Beloved to Return to You

When you have lost your love, and your loved one went to another woman, carve his name with a sharp needle into a pink candle. Also carve on it your own name. Grease this candle with jasmine oil and put it on the table. Light the wick and pronounce the spell:

> *United names, united people, joined destinies.*
> *By Fire, Earth, and Water are bound,*
> *By Sky married, conjured by spell,*
> *By deed defined, for each other forever found.*

When the candle burns out completely, collect all the remaining wax and place it in a flowerpot filled with soil. If you have hair, nail clippings, or dried blood of your loved one, mix with yours (hair, nails, blood), then bury them also in this pot. Plant a flower in the pot and, watering it every day, pronounce the familiar spell. As the flower grows and rises, the feelings and desires of the one who left you will also arise.

❋ Restore Your Relationship

If you broke up with your man not of your own free will, and you cannot restore the relationship, this ritual will help you to reunite with your beloved. Wait for the full moon, take ten candles and a porcelain cup filled with water. Place the candles around the cup, light them, focus, and speak the following charm:

The moon, always changing, you return to yourself.
Take away my sadness and woe, and crush it into powder.
Return and multiply those things that I loved most to me.
I wish [name of the man] health and a new life with me
[name],
That no one else may take him into her life.
My word is strong, mouth, tongue, lock.

Extinguish the candles and pour the water out the window. The candles can then be used at your discretion.

❋ What to Do if You Have Cheated on Your Partner

If there is an unpleasant situation with your man—namely, you cheated on him and he left you, saying that he will not forgive—you can fix it. You must conduct a special ceremony. If you want your loved one to forgive you, go home and take a shower. Then wipe your body, not with a towel but with underwear. At the same time, say the following charm:

The body is washed, sins washed away.
God forgives everyone, and you forgive me, [name], for everything
I have done.
As my body dries, so does [name] forgive me.
As my clothing dries, so no trace will remain of the insult to [name].
Amen.

Repeat this charm nine times in a row, then hang your underwear at the window to dry. Your relationship and personal life will be fine.

❋ How to Reunite with a Loved One

At first glance this charm seems to be quite simple and easy, but it has tremendous power. To carry it out, you must buy a new needle, and, holding it, speak these words:

> *I'll go out into the yard, walk along the path, and go into an open field. There's not a single tree there, nor a single bush. I'll look at the clear sky and see an arrow flying through it. This arrow will fly through the field without touching the ground, and it will strike the heart of [name]. Let it revive love in him, so that he yearns for me both day and night. Let it be as I wish; let him pine out of love. Amen.*

Afterward you must hide the needle where no one will find it. But it must be either in your home or among your lover's possessions. Since the second option is not entirely safe, it is better to hide it in your home.

❋ Restore a Beloved Relationship

If your relationship with a loved one or someone close to you has ended, the following ritual will help you: Pour a glass of clean drinking water and put it on a table. Place a candle next to it. Then take a simple black thread (about 7 inches) and tie seven knots on it. Light the candle and say:

> *I offer quarrels and strife to sacred fire, with holy water I ask for peace and love.*

Afterward, burn the thread and slowly drink the water. Then extinguish the candle and say, "Amen." Afterward, your relationship will begin to recover.

❋ Make Peace with Your Beloved

If you are in a quarrel with a loved one or a person close to you and want to make peace as soon as possible, the following ritual will help. Light a wax candle in the evening, before you go to bed, and, looking through the flame, say the following charm:

> *I let go of the pain, sadness, resentment, and irritation. I send love, peace, and harmony. Amen.*

Then go to bed. In the morning you will be able to safely meet your beloved; understanding and reconciliation are assured to you.

❊ Charm to Make Your Beloved Remember You

When a man and a woman meet and decide to form a relationship, at the beginning of this period men show unprecedented activity—they give gifts, surprise women, and surround women with care and tenderness. But in life it often happens that after some time the man begins to not pay special attention to his woman, taking more interest in his own life and affairs. Sometimes a man just disappears from the life of a woman, without explaining the reason, without warning. And the woman does not know what to think or what to do. She is lost in conjecture about what happened and what changed. In such a case there is a strong charm for the love of a man that will not let him forget about his woman.

Read these magical words in a whisper over a burning candle, holding in front of you a photograph of the person you are charming:

> *My whisper, fly to [name], go,*
> *Wake [name]'s heart, light his soul.*
> *Make [name] remember me.*
> *He will hold me in his memory as the bright sun, a beautiful woman.*
> *Let him remember me, so that he will exhaust himself to find me.*
> *Let him find me instantly, as quickly as a hunter finds his prey.*
> *Amen.*

Burn the photograph over the candle's flame and scatter the ashes at a crossroads.

❊ Remove Indifference Using an Icicle

To destroy the obstacles of indifference, coldness, and misunderstanding that have emerged between you and your beloved, put an icicle or ice cube on a small plate on top of your man's photograph (write his full name on the back). Say aloud what you want to be gone while watching it melting, imagining that's exactly how the problems and obstacles that separate you from your beloved person are disappearing. When the ice melts completely, collect all the water and add it secretly to your chosen one's drink. Put away the photograph.

SPELLS TO MAKE A MAN MARRY YOU

❋ Marriage Spell with Round Pebbles

If a man does not want to get married, and you date him or live in a common-law marriage, you can perform a special ritual to push him to this step. You must take him to the river and look together for round, smooth pebbles. You can tell him that you need it for a decoration or any reason you come up with. On the stone he finds, draw two intertwined hearts in red ink, and beneath them two intertwined engagement rings. Write *wedding* below. Bury the stone under an oak tree. Then you must hold a special ritual and write the following spell on a sheet of paper:

The icy prince is riding on a chariot of the wind,
He does not lead me to the bridal chamber.
Melt, red sun, the winter frost;
Light, bright stars, the pathway to the bridal chamber.
Blue sky, lead the prince to the bridal chamber,
That he may be betrothed to me and marry me.

Burn the paper and scatter its ashes to the wind.

❋ Kindle the Passion for Marriage

This will require a box of matches. Light a match one at a time and read the words:

My soul separates from my body, approaching Fire.
Kindle the flame of passion and love in [name]'s heart.
Let him fall to the power of my charms.
Let his thoughts be only about me,
Let his feelings push him toward a serious step,

Let him into my house.
Let it not be long before he wants to get married, that's all I ask.
There's a time for everything, a time for passion, a time for friendship,
But the time has come to create a family.
Amen.

❊ Marriage Spell with Bed Linens

If you love a man, but he does not want to get married, the magic of bed linens will help. If you think about it, bedclothes are in contact with your sleeping body and serve to transfer energy. You must buy sheets with a symbol of fertility on them, such as grapes or the sun. Use holy water to draw both his and your own name and surname. Wind three small balls of red thread and put them under the pillows. Read the following charm:

I wind this thread and conjure [name]'s heart. It is right for you to be with me, your wife, [name].

Place the pillow under the covers, below the spot where your ear would be. Put the following note into the pillow as well:

I am sweeter than honey, hotter than summer, dearer to you than any other, a kindhearted and playful woman.

Then just say:

Sweet pillow, send to my chosen one, [name], sweet dreams, so that he may sleep softly and soundly, without forgetting me.

SPELLS TO DAMPEN LOVE

❊ Cool Someone's Feelings

Cool the heat of emotions using hot metal and the grass of St. John's wort.

Light a candle, pour a steeped infusion of St. John's wort into a high goblet, and heat the blade of a knife on the fire. The metal must be red hot. During all this time, repeat in your mind the name of your former (or present) lover. Remember how earlier your love ignited and burned, just as the metal is now flaming. Imagine that all feelings and desires are concentrated on the hot tip of the knife. Lower the blade into the goblet with the infusion and say:

> *As iron has cooled, so will his, [full name]'s, feelings toward me, [name].*

Or:

> *As iron has cooled, so will passion of [full name] for [name] cool down.*

The person whose feelings you want to cool needs to drink the infusion, or if you can, put it under his doorstep.

❋ Get Rid of an Unloved Partner

If you do not know how to get rid of an annoying boyfriend whom you do not love, this charm will help to get rid of the unloved one. You must read it at the waning moon. At night, after midnight, light a candle and say:

> *On a moonlit night, I, [name], will go into a dense forest. I'll choose a thick pine tree in the forest, which I will cut into seven. I'll get a golden hatchet. Three times I will call to [name of boyfriend]. Fly, falcon, take the hatchet, cut the pine. The falcon flew in, cut and cut, until the hatchet broke. Understand that the pine was not born for you. Fly away, falcon, far away, to where no one can see you. Leave [name] alone; walk freely on your own. So be it.*

You must read the charm four times over the burning candle, once every night.

❋ Free Your Former Lover and Yourself

To free your former lover and yourself from love, throw a branch of verbena into the fire and say:

Through clear flames I conjure,
Through the pigeon grass I command
Blessed [name] to stop loving me,
Neither in thoughts, nor in reality,
Nor in a dream be with me anymore,
Her I shall forget, in day and night
Not lament or recall, remove from sight,
Forever and ever, so be it.

❊ Cool Someone's Love in an Abandoned House

To cool down the love of a person whom you find unpleasant, step up to an abandoned house where no one has lived for more than seven years. Without entering it, throw through a broken window or open door an old copper coin, and say these words:

I'll rise early, downward I'll go,
Down black path, to mouse hole
Under the sun that didn't rise,
Under the dark moon, and a night star,
Into a wide field, where dungeon hides,
Inside a crypt there, a virgin lies
As her body—her blood is still,
The heart no longer aches; sadness,
Sorrow, or breath she can't take
So would [name] for [your name]'s blood be still,
Heart would be ice cold by my will,
All grief and sadness flew beyond black hills,
Beyond the white snow, to other's lands,
Each for themselves will make amends.
So be it.

❊ To Painlessly Part with a Former Loved One

To painlessly part with the one you fell out of love with, pick a few twigs from an old broom. Finely chop them. Throw these bits between yourself and the former loved one and say:

As a broom swept dirt and dust on both sides,
Our feelings and hearts are scattered reside.
As these twigs cannot be gathered,
So we are not to be together,
In different places to live we're meant
And for each other never lament.

❋ Parting Spell

If you want to part with a man with whom you fell out of love, write his name seven times on a sheet of paper. Next to it write your own seven times. Light two black or purple candles and cut the paper in half—so that your names get separated. Burn both halves on different candles. Going out on the street or on the balcony, put the ashes from one sheet of paper onto the left palm and those from the other onto the right. After waiting for a gust of wind, blow off the ashes from the palms in different directions. If you need to separate your loved one from his mistress or lover, then write their names on the paper and then proceed in the same way.

❋ Spell to Lull Love

To lull love, pour poppy seed into a black sack. At midnight, go three times backward around the house of the person you want to charm, scattering the poppy seed directly on the ground and saying this spell:

Love fall asleep, do not wake no more.
Heart close firm, do not open your door
As this poppy cannot be gathered,
So and me with [name] will never be together.
As poppy scatters, love wastes away,
As the love has left—the road has swayed,
Heart away from heart, soul away from soul,
You away from me, me away from you.

❋ Parting Spell Using Salt and Ashes

Buy salt in three different stores and mix it with three handfuls of ashes. When you meet a man with whom you've fallen out of love, discreetly scatter between him and yourself this mixture and say:

As salt with ash doesn't merge,
So [name] with me does not converge,
Not in love, nor in the flesh;
Not in the heart, nor in the soul;
Not in reality, nor in a dream.

If your meetings are always held in public, and it isn't possible to do all this, sprinkle the salt and ash in front of his front door and say the same words.

❋ Parting Spell at a River

Go to a fast river and take a handful of earth directly from the water—as far as possible from the shore. When you see the person whom you used to love, scatter this earth between yourself and them and say:

As fast the river [name of the river] flows,
The sand rinses off the sands,
Thus me and [name] would not be together in flesh,
Not in love, nor in the heart, nor in the soul,
Nor in reality, nor in a dream.

❋ Parting Spell at Riverbanks

Go to the river and take a handful of earth from each of its opposite banks. Scatter this land between your former lover and yourself and say:

As these shores never converge,
So we will never be merged,
About each other we will forget,
In heart and soul no love will set.

❋ Spell to Curse a Man to Be Alone Forever

To curse a man to be alone forever, weave a wreath of wormwood, and as you weave, say:

The old woman is old, the girl is young,
The field is bad, but in that field everything began,
The fire comes from there,
The wormwood bush blooms there,
Grows there, that old woman prays at that bush,
They are affected by these cursed words.
The girl plucks off the wormwood,
From the wormwood she weaves,
She creates a wreath.
That wreath will bring thorny pain.
He's done for life,
He is the one whom the wreath will attack,
He will be crowned, his life will be bitter,
A cursed life.
He will be alone for a lifetime
And suffer from heartache.
As the old woman told her to do, so the girl did.
Amen.

Thrust an aspen stake into the earth (if it is possible, do so through his photo), place the wreath on it, and say:

The stake protrudes, but now [name] is crowned with a wreath,
And every woman will flee from him.
He will live alone and know the bitterness of wormwood.
Amen.

Take four pinches of dirt and throw it over everything so that the work will be fulfilled.

SPELLS TO MOVE ON FROM A FORMER LOVER

❊ Stop Your Suffering Over Love

If a loved one has left you and you suffer terribly, and you want to stop suffering and move on, buy any yellow flower and burn it on the flame of a blue candle. When the petals of the flower are completely shriveled and burned, collect them all into a small paper envelope. Also put inside it a photograph of your former lover with full name on the back of it and the request of what you want to be gone (pain, feelings). Bury the envelope in the middle of a crossroads, leave seven pennies, and depart. Rest assured that after doing so you will get rid of all your past experiences and worries.

❊ Rite for When Your Feelings Have Cooled

If your feelings have passed, you have cooled toward your man, you no longer love him, and you are afraid to say so for fear of hurting him, this rite will help. You must understand that if you stay with a man out of pity, the relationship will not be good for anyone. If he is not your man, it is up to you to decide. Do not listen to your aunt or mother; listen only to yourself. This ritual will help you decide what is important to you.

Buy eleven sewing needles from three different stores. At home, spread them out on an empty table, light seven candles around them, and, holding your hands over the needles, read the following charm:

> *I loved him, I did not love him; I did want him, I did not want him.*
> *I have not deceived myself; I have not been ruled by a bad heart.*
> *Holy saints, Mother of God, tell me the answer. Amen. Amen.*
> *Amen.*

Repeat this until your hands get tired. Then quickly sweep the needles off the table and throw them into a bowl of water. When you have done so, try to interpret the shape that appears. The feelings that you first experience are important. Your subconscious mind will decide what you need and tell you about it. You will be surprised at how wise and right this decision will be.

❋ Spell to Part with Your Former Lover

To once and for all part with your former love, and not torment them or yourself any longer, cut your joint photograph down the middle, disconnecting your images, and say:

Wolf walks the mountain, and the pike swims.
They do not talk; their ways do not cross,
They do not bear fruit, or bear any thoughts,
Issues between them will not emerge
So [names] would not converge,
They will not talk, thought will not share,
Won't produce fruit, lives will diverge,
For each other all grief will submerge.

Keep the two pieces of the cut photograph together, folding them so that your faces look in opposite directions, or immediately get rid of the half on which your ex-lover is depicted.

❋ A Charm to Move On from Your Ex-Partner

If you are dating a married man; your relationship has no prospects and you know it; or if you just have unrequited love, this is a charm that will help you to forget your lover. You should know that suppressing your feelings is useless. They will announce their presence constantly and cause you pain. You must move toward the future, not run away from the past. To help you do so, use a charm to help end the painful relationship. Read the following charm to forget your beloved over a lit candle:

As this candle burns without allowing others to approach its flame, so let my heart be toward [name], and bury him forever in the past. Amen.

Roll a small piece of the candle's wax into a ball and carry it with you.

❊ Spell to Remove Longing for a Former Beloved

If you broke up with your partner or loved one, but you feel sad for him, you are drawn to him, and you constantly think about him, this love spell will help. On a blank sheet of paper write down all the feelings that you are experiencing right now, without deceiving yourself. If you feel hurt, write it down, but do not confuse this feeling with heartache. This requires honesty and a lot of work on your part. On the morning of any Saturday, burn this paper, spread the ashes over any river or stream, and say:

God created the world in six days, and on the seventh he rested. I created my own world, I destroyed it, and in its place I will build a new one. On the seventh day of work I will rest. Key. Lock. Tongue.

Soon the longing will pass.

❊ How to Forget a Past Love

A relationship does not always end in a wedding. Many couples break apart before having time to fall in love with each other. It happens that one person's feelings fade away, and the second one has to reconcile with parting and somehow go on. And what about the other emotions, how to forget when one's heart refuses to stop loving?

A special charm may come to the rescue. Surely, you will have a photo of the loved one, either of you both or of him alone. Take one of the photos, put a small piece of black bread in front of it, and cross your arms over your chest. One important detail is that the picture must be upside down. Then, read the following charm:

The person I loved and gave all my life,
Be gone from my thoughts.
There is no place for you here now.
I'll forget about you as I have done before.
As I forgot my first steps, I learned how to speak.
I will be free from love for [name],
He will be gone from my heart and mind.
Amen.

Repeat this ritual as necessary for seven days. Immediately put the bread out to be eaten by birds.

SPOUSE AND FAMILY LIFE

❋ Refresh a Spouse's Feelings

This rite will help refresh your feelings with your spouse. Very often in families, life eats away all romance and tenderness. Quarrels and discontent become a habit with each other. To avoid this and bring new notes to the relationship where love once existed, do this ritual. Buy a gift for your beloved husband; do not spare money and time when you choose it. This is also very important. Coming home, do not rush to pack it, or give it to him. Take this gift in your hands, twist it, touch it with your lips, and say these words:

> *What I give you, my darling [name], is not this gift, but my heart. My love is still alive, so let your feelings revive again. Never leave me. As soon as you touch this object, you will become tender and affectionate and you will always love me. I am in your soul, in your heart, in your thoughts. Amen.*

Afterward, wrap the gift in beautiful paper or packing and give it to your spouse.

❋ Strengthen Your Beloved's Feelings

To preserve and strengthen your mutual feelings, place your hair and the hair of your beloved person and photos of each of you with full names written on the back (write your full name on his photograph and his on yours, so you will be inside of each other's thoughts) in a small container with honey, cinnamon, and red rose petals and say these words:

> *Like our hair, by sweetness surrounded, for centuries will*
> *be united,*
> *So will we unite, and live our life—a sweet delight.*
> *Forever and ever.*

Seal the container and keep it secret and safe. Even better: bury it in the ground in a deserted place. Until this secret is discovered and revealed, your union will be inseparable.

❊ Spell to Get Pregnant

Take an egg, not from a store but from under a chicken in the countryside, and use it to draw circles around your belly. As you do so, say:

> *The seed to the field, the field to the fruit, where the seed falls, there let the fruit grow.*

Cook this egg and eat it. Do this the day you plan to be with your husband. Repeat if it does not work the first time.

❊ Spell for a Strong and Happy Family

If you want to have a strong and happy family, perform this ritual: On the new moon, place a few small mirrors on the windowsills with the reflecting side facing toward the street. Above every one say:

> *All the evil will be reflected in you, it will not enter my house, but whoever sent it will not escape his own evil. Amen.*

The charm has a special power under the new moon. On the next new moon, repeat the ritual.

❊ Harmonization of Relations

Go to sleep on the left side of the bed, and let the husband sleep on the right. Put a pair of your husband's shoes under your side and place your shoes under his side. Read the following charm over the shoes beforehand:

> *The husband is the body, the wife is the rib. As the husband goes, the wife follows. The husband in front, the wife behind. Lord, judge each one according to his place. Amen.*

❊ Remove Relationship Curse

If a husband and wife have quarreled a great deal and it comes to a divorce, you must remove the curse on the relationship. You can determine whether there is a curse as follows. Take a button from any of the husband and wife's clothes. Then cut two thin threads of the same length. Pass one through each button and tie a knot at the end of the thread. Hang the buttons on the threads parallel to each other (for example, on a pencil). If they do not swing, there is no curse, but if they swing in different directions, then the spouses are cursed.

To remove this curse, get two candles, each in a separate candlestick. Set them on the wedding photo of the couple, light them, and say the following charm to remove the curse on the relationship:

> *Bright candles burn for a beautiful life, for harmony and love, to avoid quarrels and pain. As the candles melt, the spouses will not fight, there will be no discord.*

Then take warm, melted wax from opposite sides of each candle and put them together to make a small ball. The spouses will stop quarreling after this.

❋ Prayer against Jealousy

You trusted your beloved before you got married and had complete harmony and understanding between you, but the situation changed after the wedding. You began to control him, answer his calls, and demand a full report on what he was doing. All of this could ruin your relationship. This prayer will help with jealousy. It will strengthen your relations, relieve tension, and return the relationship to its former harmony. After all, to make things better, you must give your spouse more freedom and learn to trust him.

The prayer for jealousy is structured like a charm. It should be repeated as often as possible, preferably at least three times a day:

> *I no longer look with the eyes of a big sister,*
> *I relinquish total control, I trust my husband.*
> *I'm not his mother, but his wife,*
> *He's my support and my wall,*
> *He's the lead, I'm the led,*
> *He's the head, and I'm the neck. So be it.*

In a week of repetition of the prayer against jealousy, you will notice that your inner state changes. Your anxiety will go away, your irritability will be replaced by gratitude, and your husband will once again adore you.

❋ Remove Your Beloved's Jealousy

In so many families, wives and husbands suffer from mutual jealousy. Or conversely, one is jealous, and the other has to constantly justify himself and show evidence of his devotion. Sometimes jealousy poisons life in a marriage so much that it can lead to divorce.

This charm is ideal for those women who suffer from the jealousy of the husband. If your spouse harasses you with his suspicions and ceases to control himself, it's time to do something. To perform this ritual, you will only need your engagement ring. Remove it from your finger, and say the following:

> *The lamb is little, quiet, and calm, and you, my dear spouse, will be the same. Be sure and trust me as a best friend and as you would trust yourself. Love me as the only woman; I'm only yours and I will never betray you. Take it into your heart and do not exasperate me; I will not leave, I will not trade you for another, whoever it may be. My words will be fulfilled. Amen.*

❋ Bring Your Partner Back to the Family

If you want to bring your husband back to the family, you must perform the following ritual: Take anything your husband used (it can be something like a comb, a notebook, or some piece of clothing). After sunset, pour a few pinches of salt on the chosen item and read the following charm:

> *The salt of the earth arouses thirst in [name] for his native home, for his wife, and for the little ones, so that only one road, the road to his home, will be light and sweet to him.*

Set aside the salted item until morning. Then, at dawn, sweep up the salt, go outside, and throw it in the street. After this ritual your husband will experience an irresistible urge to return.

❋ Breakup and Reunification

If your husband left you for another, and you want him to return, a special ritual will help. You must be able to interact with the elements of Earth and connect to its strength. The ritual must be performed on the waning moon. Pour a cup of salt and whisper over it:

> *Beyond dark forests, beyond deep rivers, in a stone cave, there is a cave of serpents and dragons. They find fault with each other, bite with their teeth, sting with their stingers. As those creatures will not rest, so [name of the husband] and [name of the rival] are always quarreling. Let them fight, bite, and harm each other—let them not get along with one another. Key. Lock. Oath.*

Pour the salt out at the couple's front door.

❋ Spell against Husband Going to Mistress

If a married man gets enchanted by a young mistress, and because of this he plans to quit his family, you need to pledge these words:

I will rise at an early dawn,
Wash myself in springwater,
Into the clear fields flee
Through green meadows pass
And go straight to the sea
Sea shores stand firm on side
Do not converse, converge, or collide
So would the [name of the husband]
With the [name of the mistress] stand firm
Not have converged, conversed, or returned
From each other forever turned.

This spell should be said when a man sleeps, or read over the water in which he will wash or that he will drink.

❋ If Your Husband Is a Manipulator

If your loved one or husband begins to manipulate you, it is not good. He knows all the subtleties of psychology and is a skillful manipulator. Such people very skillfully conquer hearts, and you will not even notice how it happened. But such a family life does not bring happiness. You are constantly experiencing suffering, and you can never defend your opinion or do something without his permission. You are so afraid of offending him, but he, in turn, is never afraid of offending you, doing it often. Even if he is in the wrong, he still arranges everything in such a way that you have to approach him first and settle the conflict. And you understand that you have emotional dependence on him, but you cannot do anything about it.

From the outside your husband seems perfect, as he does not drink, does not wander, does not curse, spends money on you generously, earns well, never screams, your mother-in-law respects you, and your mother is delighted with him. But, strangely enough, such a perfect husband makes you cry constantly. You may panic at the thought of saying something wrong, so that he will not talk to you. And your husband can manage to take offense at the most incredible and simple things, and then give you the cold shoulder. And it terrifies you.

But there is a special rite to get out of the power of a manipulator. So, if your husband is a manipulator, you must find two stones, one black and one white. For seven days you must knock them over your head and repeat the following charm seven times:

> *Great Mountain, strengthen me like your immortal daughters.*
> *Harder than a stone, stronger than damask.*
> *Give me the power with which all your children are endowed.*
> *From now until my dying breath.*
> *Amen.*

On the eighth day, the stones should be hidden in a deserted place. After forty days, you should repeat the ritual. Store the stones. Already after the first stage you will feel that you begin to change. Unusual firmness and calmness will appear in you. You will react to your husband's behavior with an indulgent smile. He cannot at first understand what is happening to you, but realizing that he no longer has power over you, he will become soft as silk. And you will begin to enjoy family life and your golden husband.

SPELLS TO STOP A ROMANTIC RIVAL AND PREVENT CHEATING

❋ How to Get Rid of a Mistress

You can bring back your chosen one, who left you for your opponent, if you know her name. Light a black candle. Write your beloved's name at the top of the candle, and below his—the name of the woman. With the same needle you used to carved the names, jab the flame of the candle and say:

How flame of this fire is split,
Thus serf [name] and serf [name] will part.
Forever and ever stay apart.

Repeat this spell until it becomes obvious and clear to you that your words have become true. Then put out the candle. Split it in half with a sharp knife, thus separating the two names. Throw away these two candle parts in different places, as far apart as possible.

❋ Remove Affection of Your Beloved's Ex

If you want to save your man from excessive affection from his ex-girlfriend (who is maybe playing "love games" with your man, hoping that you will break up), perform this simple ritual. It should be done in the evening, after sunset. Take a new needle, put it on a mirror, and say:

There are not two corners for [name], but one. Until his hair goes gray he will not remember my rival [name]. As this needle is reflected into the mirror, so [name] sees only me so clearly, and so is [name] sewn to me and only me with a strong thread. Amen, amen, amen.

With this needle, sew at least a few stitches into his favorite clothes, for example, his trousers, and after a few days your loved one will forever forget about his ex.

❋ Get Your Beloved Back from Another

If the person you love has gone with another woman and you want to get him back, write on one side of an egg (buy the egg from a farm not the store) the name of your chosen one, and on the other side the name of your rival.

Imagine that the egg symbolizes their relationship and feelings. Go out and break the egg by throwing it on rocky ground.

❋ Spell against a Rival

Go to the market to buy fresh fish with the skin still on. Come home and place a photo with the full name of the rival inside the fish and start cleaning the scales while speaking these words:

I will not rise without blessing,
I'm not going to cross myself, I'm not out the door,
From the gate is not a gate,
On foot along the road,
To the River Mother!
River Mother, you are full of every fish,
Small and large,
And pike, bream, and sheefish!
I'll catch a proud fish,
Still in its scales,
She is already bending to my will,
I took her in to serve at my beck and call.
My rival is on parole!
This is not a bream, but a frolicking lover [name], and [name] a clod,
And not the head of a fish [name] but the one I have chosen,
That is not the body of the fish in the scales, but my rival [name] in their armor.

I remove scales from the fish, I strip away all my rival's protection.
I raise my sharp knife,
I cut off the head from the body,
Yes, it's not a head cut off, but the rival [name] removed from the house,
This is not the body from the head cut off, but the connection between [name] and [name] completely destroyed!

After this, take the body of the fish and bury it with the words:

As the body of the fish in the earth rots, so my rival [name] will no longer be with my chosen one!

Then take the head and also bury it while saying the words:

As this head rots, so my loved one [name] forgets my rival [name]!
As these roads do not converge, so [name] and [name] forever diverge!
My word is strong, my work is good,
My deed will not be undone. So be it!

Bury the parts of the fish on different sides of the road; read this charm once, when the moon is waning.

❋ Make Your Rival Look Old and Be Unwell

Make a woman who took your man away look old and be sick. Go to a crowded place and watch an elderly woman. Wait until she drops something, pick it up, and read the following charm over it thirteen times:

Demons of the road,
Demons of the graveyard,
Demons of the chapel,
I bow to you, I turn to you,
I enlist your support.
As from old age and disease
This old woman is weak, sick, ugly,

> *So let my rival [name] look like her.*
> *As things fall from her old hands at this moment,*
> *And as the best years have gone, vanished,*
> *So will [name]'s beauty fade away,*
> *Her youth and health will leave her.*
> *I give thirteen pennies to demons*
> *and I take thirteen months from [name].*
> *My words will not be broken.*

Perform this on a Sunday during the waning moon. You must be sure that the Sunday coincides with the day of the waning moon. This may be the most difficult part of this charm. Read this charm for thirteen nights, thirteen times each night.

Next, put the item in the same place where it was picked up. And give an offering of thirteen pennies at the crossroads. Leave the money there silently. As you return home, do not turn around and do not talk to anyone.

❋ If Your Loved One Is Cheating

If your husband or loved one is inclined to cheating or leads a wanton lifestyle but you do not want to part with him, you can use a charm against a husband's betrayal to fix the situation. To perform it, you must freeze about one cup of ice. Then you must defrost that ice and pour the thawed water into a glass. Say the following charm against a husband's betrayal over the water seven times:

> *Be gone from [name], demon, devil, unscrupulous cheat. Serpent, inferno, be gone. Return to the one who gave birth to you.*

Add the charmed water to the husband's tea or coffee, one half in the morning, the other in the evening. Repeat this ritual as necessary for seven days.

❋ Charm against Husband's Betrayal

If your husband constantly travels on business, goes on long trips, or just works long hours, and you begin to doubt his loyalty, you can cast a strong charm against a husband's betrayal. Despite the simplicity of this rite, it is very effective. Take a photo of the two of you and glue it to the pendulum on the back of a wall clock. As the clock runs, say the following charm against a husband's betrayal:

> *Wherever you are, [name], you are unable to move unfettered, but are still bound to our home.*

After this you can be calm, as your spouse will not be able to cheat on you.

SPELLS TO BREAK UP A COUPLE

❊ Breakup Spell with Nettles

Pick nettle leaves and carry them home. At home, put the leaves in a bowl and place a photo of those whom you want to quarrel under the leaves. If there is no photo, then place things belonging to the couple. If there are no ties to the couple, then say the following over the vessel:

> *On [name] and [name] let this be done. Amen.*

Put on gloves and begin to crumple, sort, throw, and pinch the leaves and say nine times:

> *Black nettles you sting, raise welts and hives. Between these two you will rise, you will not be stagnant. You are so adept, the mistress of cluttering alleys. Any thoughts you ruin, any grace you spoil. And if you notice lovers, then you eat them, you chew, you sting.*
>
> *Yes, you inspire hatred in the hearts of both. They live like you among your leaves.*
>
> *Yes, they throw themselves into your stings, they are unhappy, they scorch your black leaves.*
>
> *Yes, in the heart of [name] and [name] you enter in an absolute way, to tear them up, rip them apart, rushing to crush them. Let [name] and [name]'s kisses turn to bites and their touches leave hives. I can see words with my eyes, the black hatred of nettles.*

Yes, nettles, with the souls of beasts, will tear allies apart with a whirlpool of black hatred. You will turn [name] and [name] against each other and start them fighting like beasts, with teeth and foaming mouths.

They will gnash their teeth, tear themselves away, move away, flee hundreds of feet away. And if they spend time together, they will rage at each other like dogs. So they must live grieving, eating with screams and not with words. Then the nettles will bring hatred to [name] and [name].

You will crush them for me, tear into them, and infuse hatred into the hearts of [name] and [name]. So you irritate their quarrels with quarrels. Their mouths will foam, their teeth will gnash. Amen. Amen. Amen.

Leave everything until the nettle leaves dry. Then scatter them where the subjects live and say:

Let hives enter the feelings between [name] and [name]. Amen.

❊ Breakup Spell During the Waning Moon

Do this during the waning moon. Obtain a chicken foot and pour water into a metal basin from the tap. Light a black or inverted church candle. Take the chicken foot in your right hand. Place the foot on the surface of the water and read the following charm thirteen times, with hatred that is representative of the scenes of their scandals, quarrels, or fights:

I'm going to take a walk on a pathway, not on a road,
I'll walk sideways into a mouse's hole,
Go from there to a high mountain,
And it is on that mountain that the devil and she-devil live.
They sit, glare angrily, their teeth chatter.
The she-devil rushes to the devil, claws at him,
Black blood, they poured,
They do not agree to live together.

So let [name] fight with [name]
They will not live together.
They look at each other angrily; their teeth grind against each other.
They throw themselves, fling themselves, and spill blood.
They do not call one another by name, do not eat together, and do not sleep together.
They spit at each other, fight, and never get along in anything.
Words to words to deeds.
So be it!

Pour the water around the rival's house, preferably at the front door. Then give the foot to a stray or unknown dog and leave an offering at a crossroads (such as coins or vodka).

❋ Breakup Spell with Pine Needles

Take seven pine needles, break off the heads, and insert the needles into a spool of black thread. Bury them along with the photo of the people you want to break up. Stand in the spot where you buried them and say nine times:

When these needles grow heads once again, only then will [name] with [name] get along with each other. Amen.

Throw away the heads. Do this ritual on three days in one week: Tuesday, Thursday, and Saturday.

❋ Separation Spell with Red Pepper

Take red pepper during the waning moon and say these words:

With sorcery I call [name] and [name] to separate!

At midnight take photos of the people in question, put them together, "faces" apart, sew the photos with black thread, and use your left hand to pour red pepper between the photos and say six times:

As red pepper burns the tongue, so [name] with [name] will burn.
They cannot live together, so be it!

❋ Breakup Spell with Wax

Take two wax candles, melt them, and pour the wax into a saucer, where it should solidify. Take the third candle, light it, and put it in the middle of the solid wax. Read the following charm:

The field is waxy, yellow and dense,
It has merged into one without scattering drops.
I'll split it, half the lock: one half into a black box, another into a silver one.
I'll cast locks with heavy keys overseas.
I'll throw one box on the high mountains, in the wide valleys.
I'll throw another box into a dark, bottomless lake.
Never will those caskets be together, nor will they look at each other.
No one can find those caskets, those locks.
I have the keys, and I am the mistress of them.
While I live, I will keep them for myself:
I will not give them up, I will not sell them,
I will answer strength with force and triumphant victory.
As the casket does not merge, so the halves of the wax are not to be sealed together,
Not to merge together,
So [name] can never live together with [name].
There can be no love between them.
It is stamped heavily with black words.
This spell can neither be undone nor broken!

When the third candle burns, the contents of the saucer must be divided into two parts. The wax should be taken to the river and buried on opposite banks.

You can put a photo of a couple under the saucer. Cut it and bury it along with the different halves of the wax. It is occasionally suggested that the saucer must also be broken and buried.

❋ Breakup Spell with Onion

Cut an onion in half and write his name on one half and her name on the other. Sing as you cut the halves. Then salt the halves.

Take photos of those whom you want to quarrel, cut them out along their outlines, and stick his image to the half of the onion with her name and her image to his half. Attach nails or needles to his half, one below his picture and one above.

Put the halves back together (so that the pictures have their backs to each other), tie the onion crosswise with a black thread, and put it on the windowsill in the light of the moon. While the onion rots, the objects will be fighting one another. If it rots completely, the relationship is over. As thread is natural, it must also rot. During the day, cover it with a black cloth, a napkin, or paper. Then just bury what's left of the onion.

❊ Breakup Spell with Onion and Pepper

Take an onion and halve it evenly. Write down the names of the people whom you want to quarrel on each half with knife. Salt the onion and put cayenne and black pepper on the inside, the heart. Then, take two photos (write full names on the back) of those on whom you are casting the spell and put them back to back inside. Put them in the center of the onion, put the halves back together, and wrap it with black thread so it does not fall apart when you place it in a package or a cardboard box (not in the house). Put it in a place where it will be in the sun so it will start to rot faster and then bury it.

4 Money, Wealth, and Business Spells

The main purpose of these spells is to receive money from various sources. It includes magic that can provide a promotion at your job, career growth, help in finding treasure, contributing to higher earnings, and more. The magic of attracting wealth and good luck is very powerful and ancient magic. Luck and wealth—our ancestors used this type of magic many centuries ago; their lives became a "full bowl," and success accompanied them with their every step. The magic of wealth was used by simple people as well as military leaders in their invasions of other nations.

In the modern world, a problem such as lack of money often comes up. People, because of the inability to handle money or because of the lack of opportunities to increase income, often find themselves in a difficult financial situation, which is why even well-off families can fall apart. Every day we are faced with needs of various natures that come with financial costs. Money goes quickly, but it does not come back. You always need something; your family has become more demanding. Family members become distant and aggravated with each other because of lack of money. For such cases, there is money magic for power and wealth.

SPELLS TO GAIN WEALTH

❋ Spell to Gain Money

To perform this rite, you must gather a long, green canvas thread, a regular needle, and a church candle. In the evening, before going to bed, wrap the thread around the church candle, put it next to the bed, light it, and go to sleep while wearing a new shirt turned inside out. In the morning, get up early, at dawn. Remove the thread from the candle wax, thread the needle and stitch the underside of the shirt while you are still wearing it. But, before you do so, say the following words:

Like a thread with a needle, so does money belong with me.
As this thread is always in the needle, so money will always cling to me.
Thread is created for a needle, and a needle is needed for sewing, and money is needed for me to live.
As thread comes and goes everywhere with a needle,
So money will always strive for me and never leave me.
I'm not sewing a shirt, I'm sewing money to myself.
Coins and bills, gold and silver,
For God's grace and for good.

When the thread begins to run out, tie ten knots and cut them off. Afterward, throw the needle and the rest of the thread into any pond. Keep the shirt in your closet.

❋ Gain Money with a Magnet

To gain money, put nine of your hairs in a red flannel pouch along with a large bill and a small magnet. Keep this pouch secret and safe.

❋ Rite to Retain and Increase Your Money

If you notice that you are quickly losing your money, that it is going like water through your fingers, you must perform a powerful rite for money. You must pour cold water from the tap into a pot, add a handful of gold coins (gold-color coins or pennies) and then pour the mixture into a colander, reading the following charm for money:

The river flows; it is wide and deep. It brings much and takes no less. Take away my sorrows, river, and leave what belongs to me, what I have accumulated, what I earned with my blood. As these coins are left in the colander, so will my money be left with me. So it is.

You should leave the coins in the colander until they dry, then use them when you go shopping. Within a week you will notice a positive result: your money will begin to increase.

❊ Talisman for Wealth

A good talisman for gaining wealth can be a coin issued in the year you were born. Keep this coin in a special compartment in your wallet.

❊ Spell for Prosperity

Brooms are very powerful ritual objects. Set a clear intention for it to be your magical tool. Let's say that I want to perform a cleansing ritual in my house—when I buy that broom I will imagine that it will remove all the negative energy and sweep away enemies. Basically you put a program into this broom starting from the first moment it comes to you; you touch it and it already has a mission and purpose. When using a newly purchased broom for the first time in the house, say the following words:

Let all the good come to my house and let all the bad be gone.

This will bring prosperity and good fortune to your home.

❊ Increase the Chance for Unexpected Money

To increase the chance that you will receive unexpected money, go to an open field. There, build a small fire. Put dry wormwood, a strand of your hair, a cut nail from the thumb of your right hand, a bird feather, a clover leaf, a lock of black cat fur, and a folded note detailing the amount of money you wish to receive into a bowl. Fill the bowl with milk and put it over the fire. When the milk boils, pour it and all the other contents into a hole that you have dug. Fill the hole and say:

> *I bring this sacrifice to the lord of the earth and the underground, that it may grow in my house and in my purse. The words are said, the deed is done, all is settled. So be it!*

❋ Spell to Always Have Money in Your House

To always have money in your house, hide four new shiny coins minted in a non–leap year under the threshold in four corners of your house and say:

> *Gold to gold, silver to silver, money to money to this threshold in this house.*

❋ Improve Your Financial Situation

To improve your financial situation, write the amount of money you want to receive on a piece of paper. Fold the paper three times, add to it one dollar bill, and bury it in a flowerpot filled with earth taken from three crossroads. Plant in the pot either geraniums or marigolds. As the flowers grow, so will your wealth.

❋ Coin Talisman

Take twelve coins of the same denomination, minted only in even and leap years. After the sun sets, hold all the coins in the palms of your hands. Shake them so that they move freely and roll over the palms. Then open your hands and throw the coins in front of you on the table. Put aside all the coins that landed on tails. Gather those that landed on heads, shake them in your hands, and throw them on the table again. In the same way, set aside the coins that landed on tails and gather the ones that landed on heads. Repeat these steps until you have only one coin left. Wrap it in red cloth and store it as a monetary talisman.

❋ Money Spell with Wheat Sprouts

Place seven pennies on a simple saucer with no images on it. Pour wheat grains over them and cover the saucer with a handkerchief. Water the saucer's contents every three days with warm water to make the wheat sprout. As you water it, say:

Mother Wheat, you feed young and old, poor and rich.
From a single grain you sprout ten, fifteen, twenty stalks.
Give me, [your name], money to grow as this wheat grows.
As it grows day and night, without succumbing to hunger's blight,
So let my money grow and nourish me.
Praise the lord. In the name of the Father, the Son, and the Holy Spirit. Amen.

❋ Enchanted Coin Bank

Place a pinch of sugar and a pinch of dry basil or yarrow in a green bottle. Put three drops of bergamot oil or tincture of eucalyptus into the same bottle. Every day add one coin to the bottle. Keep this bank in your home or where you do business.

❋ Money Charm with Coins in Pouch

If you want to improve your financial situation, gather coins of different denominations, from pennies to dollars, and place them in a pouch. Be sure to use coins that are currently in circulation. Spread eucalyptus oil over each coin separately. As you do so, say the following charm:

A penny to a penny, five pennies to five pennies, a dollar to dollar, a dime to a dime, all to my coffers.

Hide this pouch in the northern part of your house.

❋ Money Spell Penny Talisman

Light a candle, pour clean water in a shallow bowl, and throw a penny into it. Drip the melted candle wax into the water directly on the coin and say:

As how the soft turns to the hard, so my wealth will grow and grow. From day to day, from week to week, from year to year, from this moment to the end of time.

Afterward, pour the water on the ground and store the coin in your purse as a monetary talisman.

❋ Money Spell During the Waxing Moon

This rite is held during the waxing moon, ideally on a Thursday. You will need pure springwater directly from a spring. At dawn pour the water into a cup, put it on a windowsill, and, placing your face close to the water so that your breathing stirs it, say three times, "Our Father," a prayer to Saint Nicholas, and these words:

> *Over Mount Sinai, over the Egyptian Earth, the Mother of God went. She collected dewdrops, brought them home, and helped [name]. This house became a full cup, not yours, but ours. With the help of God, we have joy, and no one is envious. Multiply, wealth, multiply and grow. For joy, for good, so that the world is bright for everyone. Amen.*

Then use this water to wash your hands and then sprinkle it in all the corners of your house, starting from the threshold and moving clockwise. Ensure that no one sees you do this.

SPELLS FOR STEALING LUCK

❋ To Steal Luck from a Rich Man for Yourself

Get the shirt of a rich man somehow. Tie it in a knot, put it under a pillow, and sleep on it for three days. Then luck will come to you. As you tie it up, say:

> *As I bind myself with a good knot, I create a dark fate. I'll create a black destiny with a devil below me and a dead man above. For the gentleman it no longer works, but it grows stronger.*
> *Amen.*

After the third night, take the shirt and burn it at the edge of the forest (at the crossroads will also work). When it burns, say:

> *Let the spirit diverge into a non-noble, then it will be blown to me in the ashes. Amen.*

You must wait for nine days before meeting the man whose luck you took away.

❊ Steal Someone's Luck from Home

You may steal a man's luck if you have access to his home. Take something that belongs to him, preferably an item of clothing. Say:

> *Whatever I steal will go unnoticed, by the caw of a crow, as the devil knows. Amen.*

When you arrive at home, put what you have stolen in a secluded place, so that no one finds it. Say:

> *Taken, stolen, gathered together in my house. I took his fortune, his money, everything. I am the one who took it, I'm a thief, and he is the one paying. Amen.*

❊ Spell for a Luck Thief

This is what a luck thief will do when he has no luck. He must go to a rich house and collect the dust and rubbish near it. Then he must say:

> *This is not dust, nor mud, it is luck and money.*
> *I collected all this, took it in my arms,*
> *It is good, golden, studded with gold.*
> *I took his life for myself.*
> *How will I measure my way home?*
> *My footsteps will be covered in these riches.*
> *Amen.*

He will pull it all out at his doorstep and immediately outside the threshold of his house. As he does so, he must say:

> *I went around in circles, my shovel beside me. Now I am in my hut, not for a day, but forever. Amen.*

He must let the dust lie for seven days. Then he must sweep it up, tie it in a rag, and store it in any corner of his house.

❊ Steal Wealth, Success, Luck

This ritual is to steal wealth, success, or luck from someone.

First, purchase something to make an offering: money, meat, or whatever you think is necessary. Then, the night before you wish to perform the stealing spell, go to the crossroads at midnight. Put your offerings on all four roads and say:

> *Devil, I'm calling on you to make a deal. Witness me stealing [what you will ask].*

Then you turn around (if you have coins, throw them over the shoulder) and go home as usual without looking back or talking to anyone.

The next day, perform the stealing spell in a crowded place, where there are many people. Look for the person you are going to steal from right away. Follow that person. You must walk so that you completely copy the gait of the person. That is, step by step, movement by movement. You must completely become this person. Look at the person's back between the shoulder blades. As you do so read the following charm:

> *A woman (or man) was walking with a pouch and an empty pot.*
> *The pouch is full but has a hole in it.*
> *The devil is behind her (him).*
> *Each good thing that falls through the hole, the devil picks up.*
> *The devil has a full bag, and the woman (or man) has an empty pot.*
> *So I'm this devil [your name] for you, whatever your name is, and I am coming.*
> *I take your [what you will take].*
> *The first step is to start, the second is to pick, the third is to seal it.*
> *Step by step, pinch by pinch*
> *To me, [my name], [what you will take] the bag will come.*
> *To you, whatever your name is, an empty pot will come.*
> *To me [my name] [for example: to be good and young, to prosper and grow rich, to be healthy]*
> *To you, whatever your name is, [for example: wither and die, go broke and be poor, hurt]*
> *For ever and ever.*
> *As the devil is my witness, so this will come to pass.*
> *Amen.*

Spit in front of you in the person's footsteps and stamp it with your left foot. Go home without talking to anyone or turning around.

SPELLS TO FIND TREASURE

❋ Treasure Charm Using a Blue Candle

To find treasure, make a blue candle. Place it in a candlestick carved from a walnut tree and shaped like a horseshoe. When you arrive at the place where the treasure might be buried, light the candle and, holding the ends of the horseshoe with two hands, walk back and forth around the area, uttering the following charm:

One does not search with fire in the daytime, but will find something,
One does not look with fire in the daytime, but will notice something,
One does not see with fire in the daytime, but will understand.

The closer you are to the treasure, the more the flame will die down. If it suddenly goes out completely, then you have happened upon where the treasure is buried. You can also find anything you lose in the house or yard in this way.

❋ Treasure Charm Using a Green Candle

As you arrive where rumors say that the treasure is buried, light a green candle. Pour holy water into a large bowl, look into it, and repeat the following charm:

Open the secret hidden in the belly of the earth, through the holy water, through my work, through my words. Everything that a human hand has lodged in the earth will be reflected in my bowl, the place determined, the sign confirmed.

Sooner or later you will notice that the water in the cup seems to turn into a mirror, and in it you will see the exact place where the treasure is buried. Plant a laurel branch in the soil on one side of that place. To the west, plant a verbena branch and water them with holy water from your bowl. Dig up the ground between these branches. When the hole you dig is half a human's height, make a wreath from the branches and put it on your head. After a couple of movements, the treasure will reveal itself to you, and the spell you cast on it will not harm you in any way.

SPELLS TO WIN MONEY

❊ Win Money by Gambling

To win in gambling establishments, write the amount of money you want to receive on a small sheet of paper. Fold the paper three times and put it into a small vessel that is then filled halfway with black peppercorns. Before the game begins, shake the vessel in your left hand. Envision it giving you the special power to attract luck and fortune.

❊ Win Money

To have a win, grind black pepper and cinnamon in a mortar and scatter the powder in the corners of your house and around your bed. Pour one pinch of this powder into your wallet.

❊ Charm to Bring into a Casino with You

Write the amount you want to receive in red ink on a green sheet of paper. Before you go into a gambling establishment, burn the paper and pour the ashes under the insole of your left shoe.

❊ Talisman for Good Luck in a Game

To have good luck in a game, carry a magnet, a cat's-eye stone, aquamarine, beryl, angelica root, a shark's tooth, or a piece of alligator skin in your left pocket. In addition, you can tuck a lock of white cat fur under the insole of your left shoe.

❊ Talisman for Gambling

Cut the bottom off a large bald goose feather. Pour plantain seeds into the hollow cavity. Seal the hole with white candle wax. Keep this talisman with you when you play cards, roulette, or bet on races and you will always have prosperity and profit.

❋ Talisman for Winning at Cards

If you plan to play cards, then remove a jack from an uninvolved deck of cards. Write the amount of money you want to win on the back of the card. Place the card in a small vessel or pouch filled with black peppercorns. Keep this talisman with you while you play.

SPELLS FOR BUSINESS SUCCESS

❋ Success in a Goal

To achieve an important goal, cut holes through nine beans. String all the beans on a green string and store the amulet in your house. In the morning, run your hands over the beans like you would a rosary and think about what you must do that day.

❋ Talisman for Your Desk at Work

Tie together three heads of wheat with a yellow thread and say:

Work to work, money to money, let everything come to me.

Keep this simple talisman in your desk drawer at your place of business.

❋ Spell for Everything to Go in Your Favor

To make sure everything is decided in your favor, burn the feather of a black bird over the flame of a yellow candle and say:

I call with fire, call with air, from earth to heaven, from heaven to earth, everything into my power, everything in my favor.

❋ For Good Luck in Business

To have good luck in business, mix together dry shredded herbs: use equal parts yarrow, St. John's wort, and sage. Spread a white tablecloth on a table. Place a candle on the table and light it. Take the herbal mixture you have prepared and sprinkle it over the candle's flame three times, each time uttering the following charm:

As these herbs burn, so my dealings will go to my advantage.

Say what you want clearly. Collect all the herbs that have fallen on the tablecloth and put them in the pockets of your clothes.

❋ Spell to Make Petition Go in Your Favor

When you go to a government office or any other place where you make petitions, before you go in, grab the door handle and say:

As I open this door, so all things will open for me.

❋ Charm for Success in Business

For success in business, pick up a red wool thread and say:

What I think will come to be; what I say will take place; what I do will lead to better things.

Tie a knot on the string and continue the charm:

As this knot is tied precisely and correctly, so my business will go forward precisely and correctly.

Put the thread under the threshold of your front door and go about your business in full confidence that everything you do that day will go your way.

❋ Before a New Undertaking or Business

Any new undertaking or business will be successful if you awaken before sunrise and go to an open field or climb a hill with a white feather in your right hand. As the sun's rays first appear, blow the feather away and say:

From the north and the east, from the south and the west, everything I have, everything in my path, will work for my good and joy.

❋ Spell to Hold On to Good Luck

To hold on to good luck, light red, yellow, and green candles and tie three knots in a white wool cord. When you tie the knots, say what you want over each one. Tilt each candle over and seal each knot with a drop of melted wax. Keep this rope wherever you conduct business.

❊ Success in Business and Trade

To attract customers and increase profits, drill holes in three nutmeg seeds and string them on a green thread. Tie the ends together with a triple knot. Hang the resulting "necklace" over the door of your business.

❊ Attract Customers and Protect Your Business

To attract customers, as well as to prevent theft from your business, chop fresh basil leaves and put them into boiling water. When the water cools down, sprinkle the infusion over the threshold of your store or office and around the entire building in which you conduct your business. Inside the building, you must spray a cinnamon infusion.

❊ Attract Customers to You, Repel Customers from Competitor

Mix powdered sugar with yarrow herb. Sprinkle a few pinches of this mixture in front of the threshold and around your office or trading stalls, hotels, and so on. If you have a competitor, scatter powdered lawn grass mixed with baking soda around his office.

❊ Talisman to Increase Profits

Herbs and flowers to increase profits include snapdragon, clover, dill, and ash bark. Mix them all in equal parts in a small green bag and read the following charm:

> *What I think will come to pass; what I say will take place; what I do will bring me profit.*

Hang this talisman in the place where you do business.

❊ Protect Your Career Prospects

If you are aware that someone is envious and ready to do anything to prevent you from getting a high post, always carry a black tourmaline gemstone with you. At the beginning of each day, apply a drop of bergamot oil on this stone to activate the stone's protective properties. During the day, touch the stone from time to time to gain additional strength from it.

❋ Spell to Influence Your Supervisors

Before talking with disgruntled management, read a charm over a crow's feather and hide it in the inner pocket of a jacket. You must read the following charm:

> *Crows flew through the dark sea. Seven crows grew numb and stiff. All the commanders and chiefs in front of me will become too numb and stiff to speak, so that I may speak, and they will do my will. My word will be stronger than water, higher than mountains, heavier than gold, and stronger than stone. So be it!*

❋ Talisman to Support Your Authority

If you are the director of a bank or a factory, or the owner of a large trading store, keep a cedar cone full of nuts in your office. This cone will become a good talisman, supporting your power and authority.

❋ Success in Finding a Job

If you are looking for a job and cannot find it or if you are called in to interview but are then denied for unknown reasons, that means your energy in this area is blocked. You can cope with this problem using this special ritual as a charm to get a good job. In the evening during a waxing moon, sit on the shore of a river and tie seven red threads on your right wrist. As you tie each knot, read the following charm:

> *Seven winds, seven whirlpools, seven springs. I call to you seven times and ask that you open the doors, to let [name] pass through the seven gates. From the gates of sorrow, grief, fatigue, anxiety, separation, despair, disharmony to the gate of brightness and the palace of happiness, growth, fortune, togetherness, and harmony.*

Only remove these threads the next morning. Take them to the same riverbank and read the charm once more. You will see that the next interview is successful.

❊ Spell to Make Your Business Flourish

This rite must be performed when a young moon appears in the sky. After midnight, fill a glass with clear and pure water and bring it to your lips. Read the following words over the water so that your breathing lightly stirs it:

I am [name], I ask you, water, to help me gain wealth.
Let it be as I planned and let all my plans come true.
Let my business flourish and bring me profit, that I may be happy.
Saints, come to my aid, guide me to the right path and bless my further actions.
My business is difficult, but important. Amen.

You must drink the water in small sips. During this process, mentally draw behind you the wings that will protect you so that they bring you success and luck. Repeat this ritual for seven days. Once those seven days pass, you will acquire strength, energy, and great self-confidence. The business will begin to grow larger and stronger.

❊ Spell for a Person to Be Fired from Work

Buy salt and poppy seeds, take three large pinches of each, and mix them with a knife. Say seven times:

Through the barriers, doors, and windows,
I creep out like a black viper,
To [name] I send tears, distress, and enmity,
I mix the salt with the poppy.
The salt for grief, the poppy for tears.
I craft a dirty trick and a threat for [name],
I close it with a key, I throw the lock into the sea!
No one will break my work, no one can undo it!
So it is and so it will be, thrice strong!

Sprinkle the mixture in every corner of the enemy's office, on his desk, on and under his threshold. Then pour out a path from the office to the street and discard the remnants in the opposite direction from the building. Spit three times.

❋ Spell for a Debtor to Return Money

If you are concerned about repayment of money that is overdue from a person who owes you, then you can conduct one very effective ritual. When you speak the charm you do not need to mention the name of a particular person. It will find the debtor unaided; believe in it.

Perform the ritual on a Saturday night during a full or waxing moon. Gather two candles, green and yellow; jasmine incense; and honeysuckle, nutmeg, and orange oils. You will also need crystals, a piece of green paper, plus a glass bowl (you can substitute a metal bowl).

When everything is ready, place the crystals in front of an altar. Write on the piece of green paper exactly the amount of money that is owed to you. If you want it to be returned as soon as possible, then write the following sentence:

> *My debtors always pay their debts on time, because they are honest people. Let what belongs to me return to me on time, without delay.*

Put this note on the altar under one of the crystals. Light the incense. Then you must oil the candles from wick to base with all of the oils and put them in the center of the altar. First you must light the green candle, and then light the yellow. You must burn the note, folding it several times and putting it over the flame, then pour the ashes into a bowl. While this sheet of paper burns, do not forget to say this special charm:

> *I draw to myself what should be mine by right, what belongs to me. Let all that is mine come back to me. I do not need anything else. I want and must receive what I once gave.*

Let the candles burn out completely.

❋ Protect Your Business from Sorcery

If your business is failing and you suspect that the reason for this is sorcery (someone put curse on you), you need to smudge your office with smoke of laurel and cinnamon. Grind laurel leaves and cinnamon root separately. Pour each powder on a separate plate, sprinkle them with a few drops of wine, and set them on fire. When the alcohol burns and the powders start to smoke, take the plate with laurel in your right hand and the one with cinnamon in your left hand and walk around all the rooms of your office.

SPELLS TO MAKE DEALS AND WIELD INFLUENCE

❊ Talisman to Gain Someone's Support

Obtain the hair of someone whose support you want or whom you want to see in the ranks of your allies and companions. Put the hair in the bottom of a small cup or saucer. Place your own hair in the same cup. Light a candle and tilt it over the cup so it drips melted wax on the combined hair. In this way, burn the entire candle and store the wax-filled cup in a secret place as a talisman for the success of your plans.

❊ Spell to Influence Someone for a Good Deal

To ensure that your work with a companion is especially beneficial, serve them tea, then after they leave your home or office, mix the tea leaves from their cup and yours. Dry the mixture and put it in a matchbox. When you meet with this person again, keep this box next to you. This will help you make a good deal, get a loan, or change this person's mind.

❊ Spell to Convince Others to Make a Deal

To convince partners and companions that your proposal is profitable, mix equal parts bergamot, sandalwood, and basil oils. Apply one drop of this mixture to the door handle of your office so that everyone who opens your door is affected by the mixture's magic and does not leave without making a deal. Of course, after applying the oil, the door handle needs to be cleaned well with a cloth so that it is not sticky and greasy.

❊ Spell for Successful Negotiations

As you prepare for negotiations with partners and allies, crush a dried fern root into powder while saying:

> *Let the wisdom and the strength of the herbs of the forest guide me. Mother Earth grew them, infusing in them her sacrament for wealth, for profit, and for my dream.*

As you sit at the negotiating table, discreetly scatter three pinches of this powder at your feet. Scatter one pinch to the right, the other to the left, and the third directly in front of you.

❋ Protection from Negativity during Negotiations

Before starting negotiations with your companions, smudge the room in which you are to conduct business using smoke from dried fern leaves. Hold the censer in your left hand and utter the following charm:

> *I invoke all the powers of heaven, all the earthly powers, all the powers of the air to my aid and protection. Blur the mind and thoughts of all those around me so that those against me will be weak and helpless. They will not outstrip me by word or deed; they will do as I wish and speak with my words. What I think will come to pass, and what I say will take place.*

❋ Spell to Gain Advantage over a Competitor

To obtain an advantage over an enemy or competitor, write their name on black earth. Throw an ax in the air so that, as it falls to the ground, it cuts directly through the inscription. Walk around the ax three times clockwise, then take it out of the ground and keep it in your house, secret and safe. You can also use a knife.

❋ Wielding Influence over People

To make a person change their mind and act to your benefit, take their photo and walk it around in a circle, counterclockwise, with the back of the photo facing forward. As you do so, say the words:

> *Back to front, in reverse, you will walk, you will think, you will do everything as I wish, everything as I say.*

If you do not have a photograph of the person whom you need to influence, use a piece of paper with their full name written on it instead.

❋ Potion to Influence Someone

If you want to influence a person, prepare a magical potion. Once you have it, rinse your hands in it and touch the person whom you wish to influence (shake their hand, pat them on the shoulder, etc.).

Prepare the potion as follows: Gather five pinches of dried and powdered stinging nettle leaves, three pinches of earth from a crossroads, one black feather, a lock of red cat fur, three pinches of black pepper, a pinch of salt, and one teaspoon of honey. Place these ingredients in a pot of boiling water, then remove it from the heat. When the water cools down, strain the infusion.

❋ Sweeten Your Supervisor's Decision

If your fate will be decided by someone else, such as your boss or manager, write their name on a sheet of paper nine times. Do this for nine days in a row, using the same sheet, so that the number of names on the paper totals eighty-one. Roll the paper into a tube and put it in a bottle. Fill the bottle with sugar, seal it with a stopper, and store it in your house.

❋ Influence Your Supervisor's Determination of Your Fate

Write the full name of the person deciding your fate on a sheet of paper. Write your full name on top of theirs. Wrap the sheet of paper around a long nail and tie it securely with a red thread so that it cannot move. Go to a deserted place and drive the charmed nail into the ground. Do not speak to anyone on your way home.

❋ Using Your Aspirations to Sway a Decision

Write your aspirations and desires on a piece of paper, then burn the paper. Collect all the remaining ash and add some of it to the food or drink of the one who decides your fate. If you do not have the opportunity to do this, pour some of the ashes into their left shoe. If that is not possible, then sprinkle all the ashes where your benefactor usually spends their time.

❊ Spell to Have Power over Someone Using Ashes

To have power over someone, write their name on a piece of paper, burn it, and rub the ashes on the soles of your shoes. You can use a photo of the person instead of a piece of paper.

❊ Spell to Have Power over Someone Using Paper

To have power over someone, you must write their name on a piece of paper. Fold this paper three times and wear it under the insole of your left shoe. Use a photo of this person if you have one, as it will be more effective.

❊ Influence Someone Who Holds Your Fate

Find a small, flat stone and imagine that it is the person on whom your fate hinges. As you return home and step over the threshold, throw the stone on the floor. Kick it with your left foot so that it rolls into the western corner of your house. Let the stone remain there until you get what you desire.

SPELLS TO HELP YOU WIN IN COURT

❊ Amulet to Win in Court

If you will be a defendant in court, drill a wide, deep hole in a chestnut, but do not pierce it through. Grind dry sage and tobacco into a powder. Pour this mixture into the hole in the chestnut and seal the hole with black candle wax. In court, keep this amulet with you and from time to time touch it with your left hand.

❊ Herbal Infusion to Win in Court

Prepare an infusion by boiling burdock root and psyllium seeds in water. Strain it and pour it into a glass bottle, sealing it with a cork. Keep this infusion in a dark place until the eve of the day when you will have to appear in court. When this time comes, light an orange candle and pour half of the infusion into your bath. While in the water, envision winning the lawsuit. Feel the power of magical herbs pouring into you and making you able to triumph under any circumstances. The next day, before going to court, read the following charm:

I went out the door and went through the gate to the east side. On the east side there were gold keys, silver keys, and diamond keys. I washed off those three keys, and once they were clean I saw that they had the gold of the sun, the bright silver of the moon, and the diamond sparkle of the stars. All that I say will be respected, my words will be accepted on faith, but those who are wicked and work against me will not be noticed or heard. So be it!

❋ If There Is a Charge against You

If a charge is being prepared or plans are being made against you, hold three coins in your left fist and speak the following charm:

I'll leave my house through the doors. I'll go from the doors through the gate to green fields, into clear meadows, into dark forests, to where there are thirty coffins, thirty dead. As those corpses' hearts do not beat, hands do not move, mouths do not open, so will my foe [name]'s heart not beat, hands will not move, mouth will not open. Whoever wishes and dares to hold me in their thoughts, I will rip and devour. I have a wolf's mouth, iron teeth, a bear's claws. Judgment by judgment, age by age, there is no judgment and will not be any judgment against me in the eyes of the Lord. My words are strong, and my deeds are free.

Once you go out into the street, freely give the coins as a donation to one person. Then, boldly go about your business or deliver your argument in court.

❋ Spell to Win a Lawsuit

To win a lawsuit, resist ill-wishers, or defeat your enemies, get a large red pepper and remove all the seeds from it. Write the names of all your rivals and competitors on a piece of paper. Fold the paper and put it inside the pepper. Put this pepper in an icy place and keep it there until all your negotiations and disagreements are resolved in your favor. (Ice is always used in magic to cool a person or freeze them.)

❊ If You Committed a Crime

If you were in a difficult situation and went, as they say, down the wrong path and committed a crime, then a prayer before the court will help you to resolve the situation. Know that there are always ways out of a difficult situation. You may have chosen a crooked path for good reason; you are in danger of self-destruction. Everyone is worthy of forgiveness, but you must first forgive yourself. Your inner God has already forgiven you. Accepting yourself with all your shortcomings will help you to embark on the correct path.

If you are facing a court case, then use a charm to move the judge to be merciful. This prayer before the court will help mitigate the punishment. When the hearing begins, say to yourself three times:

> *The judge closes the door, but God opens it. God, who dwells in the judge's heart, let mercy temper his strict demeanor. Amen.*

❊ Sweeten the Judge

On the eve of an important day, write the name of the judge or the person who will decide important matters on a piece of paper. Put the paper on a plate with your request and put a piece of ice on top of it. Carve a hole in the ice and put sugar in it. Then, place nine candles around the plate and light the wicks. Watch as the ice melts and envision that the heart of the judge whose name you wrote melting in the same way. Imagine that you will be able to "sweeten the situation" and that in the long run you will get what you desire.

❊ Defeat Your Enemies

A heliotrope stone worn in your left pocket will help you win a lawsuit and defeat your enemies. To activate the properties of this stone, apply three drops of bergamot or rosemary oil or throw it into boiling water infused with rose petals or rosehips.

❊ If You Need to Sue for Justice

If you have a situation in your life in which you must sue to obtain justice, you can cast a charm for a fair trial. To do this, you must charm the clothes you will be wearing in court. Before court you must sprinkle charmed water over your clothes. Take a glass of clean drinking water, put it on the threshold of the front door, and let it stand for thirty minutes. Then say the following charm:

> *[Your name], a prince and a merchant, will go to the people's court, good fellow that he is. In court he will have luck and victory. So I have said, and so it shall be. Amen.*

After you sprinkle water over your things, pour what remains outside. You will find that the court will rule in your favor.

5

Protection Spells

Protection spells are one of the many branches of magic. People perform protection spells when they want to save something important or ensure that something won't be lost. Historically, many military leaders and kings used magic to protect their countries and nations.

The magic of protection is divided into several areas: protection of health and life; protection of relationships; protection from the evil eye, damage, and other negative energies; protection and preservation of property; protection of business from competitors; as well as individual methods of protection.

SPELLS TO COUNTERACT CURSES AND THE EVIL EYE

Spell against Curses or the Evil Eye

To protect against curses and the evil eye, collect and dry these protective herbs and plants: St. John's wort, clover, wormwood, tansy, thistle, and sage. Mix them all together, saying:

> *Herbs with herbs unite against dark forces, filling up with bright light for [your name] to take hold of.*

Sew a small pouch out of red cloth and fill it with the herbal mixture you made. Sew the pouch closed so that the herbs do not spill out. Wear it on a red cord around your neck.

❋ Protect from Negative People

It is not always possible to let only friendly people in your home; sometimes you have to see negative people as well. This charm will protect you from curses and the evil eye in such a situation. Usually after this type of guest visits, everything starts to break down, things get lost, and the family quarrels for no reason.

To avoid all this, you can perform a simple ceremony. If it is winter, break off any icicle outside, quickly bring it into your house, and use it to draw seven crosses on your doorstep. If it's a warm season, tear a dry branch from a tree to suit your purpose. As you draw the crosses, read the following charm to ward off the curse of the evil eye:

> *Covetous eyes are demons; they eat away at your soul. As this water froze, so will your envy grow cold. Whoever passes over these seven crosses will fall under the effects of this seal. Key. Lock. My word.*

Throw the icicle (or branch) outside over your left shoulder.

❋ Close Yourself Off from the Evil Eye

While tying your shoelaces, buttoning buttons, putting on a ring, or pinning on a brooch, say mentally or aloud:

> *I close myself off to evil deeds, from the evil eye, and from wicked words, to ensure you have no access, not on the road, at work, or at rest. Not at night, nor during the day. These words are my lock and key, now and forever.*

❋ Spell to Protect against Dark Magic

Light white and black candles. Take the black candle in your left hand and the white one in your right hand. Stand in front of a large mirror in which you can see yourself from head to foot. Say:

Between these two candles, between these two lights there is not and there will not be dark magic, evil will, or cursed thoughts. So it is said, and so it will be.

❊ Protection from Harm

When the sun is hidden beyond the horizon, place eight candles in a circle and light them. Stand in the circle of candles and say the following charm:

In this dark night, I invoke the sacred power of fire to protect me from anything that can cause me harm, whether spiritual, emotional, mental, or physical. By the power of my word, by the strength of my desire, by the force of my will, so be it!

Envision the wall of fire surrounding you on all sides. Feel the sacred flame burning away all the evil and harm that lays in your path and surrounds you.

❊ Spell against Curses and Jinxes

Speak the following words over a lump of salt:

To everyone who seeks to curse or jinx me, let them have salt in their eyes, hot sand from burning fire! Such people are not recognized by God. Clouds do not open for them, bright stars do not break through, there is no dawn in the morning sky, and the moon is hidden away. By my words, by my name, [name], do not hurt, do not harm, do not destroy, do not devour, so be it!

Carry a few pinches of this salt in your pocket.

❊ If You Feel an Evil Force from Someone

If you feel an evil force coming from someone, mentally draw the cross on this person. Do this three times and, without opening your mouth, say to yourself:

By this cross, cover this person so that he thinks no dark thought, does no evil deed, and fixes no wicked gaze on others.

As you communicate with such a person, keep your right hand in your pocket and hold a fig in your hand.

❊ Protection Spell Using a Mirror

If you have a round mirror hanging in your house, you can use it to protect yourself from evil. Remove the mirror from the wall. Put it in the center of the table and surround it with eight candles. Light one of the candles and say:

I set out to deflect evil and bring peace.

From the flame of the first candle, light the second wick and repeat this charm. Do the same with all the other candles. Look at the candle lights reflected in the mirror and say:

Around and within the forces of evil, be as a shield. Conjure one to eight from around the world, eight incarnations.

Then extinguish the candles and return the mirror to its original place. Now all the evil eyes and cruel words spat and uttered in your house will not do harm to you or your loved ones.

❊ Protect All Who Live in the House from Curses

To protect all those who live in your home from curses, evil eyes, and dark spirits, pass a white thread half a foot in length through the eye of a needle. Tie the ends of thread together with a triple knot. Swipe the tip of the needle around the door frame, then stick it into the top of the door frame above the top door hinge and say:

This needle will stand on guard to defeat all enemies.

❊ Protect Your House from Dark Forces

To protect your house from dark forces, with white thread tie two long needles together in the middle, forming the shape of a cross, and say:

Crossed spears, all enemies bowed. Anyone who thinks well and with good intentions will pass through, but those corrupted by evil will be blocked by the cross.

Hang this talisman directly above the front door inside the house or hide it behind the door's outer trim.

❊ Amulet to Forget Suffering

To create an amulet, you will have to catch two small spiders in your house and place them in a walnut shell. Firmly tie it with black thread. The thread should be thick and the halves of the nut should be closely pressed against each other. When you tie the thread, say the following words:

> *I will lose this amulet, so I will forget about my suffering. I am protected, now and forever.*

As soon as you lose this little amulet, the affliction will go away. But you cannot throw it away deliberately. You must forget that you have it, and then it will disappear.

❊ Spell against Wicked Thoughts and Deeds

Fill a small glass bottle to the brim with small nails, needles, or pins. Seal the bottle with a cork and hang it in the northern corner of your house or in the hallway above the front door and say:

> *Neither near, far, nor high; neither low, deep, nor wide; neither narrow, broad, nor anything else;*
> *No way, no how, no word, no deed, no thought, not me, not you, not him.*
> *All must move, cross themselves, shift from back to front and front to back.*
> *Dark thoughts by my words will be gone! Evil tongues will cleave to iron! Wicked deeds will not be accomplished in a century!*

❊ Eliminate Enemies, Bad Spirits, and Evil

Place three small nails in a door that faces the street so that their heads form an equilateral triangle that points upward (one nail at the top, two at the bottom). After that, go into the house, close the door, and say:

> *There are three nails in this door. The first nail, to eliminate all enemies; the second nail, to exterminate all negative and bad spirits; the third nail, to drive away all evil. By all my words, the deed will be done; by all three nails, it will turn in my favor.*

❋ Keep Evil Out of Your Home

To keep evil out of your home, prepare a thick infusion of dill or thistle. Using a whisk made up of white, black, and ruffled chicken feathers, sprinkle this infusion on the front door, as well as at all the windowsills.

❋ Annual Spell against the Evil Eye

Curses and the evil eye affect a person much more often than it may appear. The worst part is that you may not even know that someone is hurting you. Therefore, it is better to secure yourself beforehand, without waiting for serious consequences. This prayer against the evil eye and curses will help you to do so.

Perform this ritual once a year. You must take a handful of whole peas to a churchyard. Standing behind the church where no one will see you, throw peas one by one against the church wall so that they bounce as far as possible. As you do so, read the following prayer against the evil eye and curses:

> *The black crow looked at St. Nicholas, cawed and pecked at him. But the worker of miracles remained intact and unharmed. The black cow mooed at Saint Helena and left a trace of its tongue upon her. But the virtuous woman remained unharmed. The black hyena laughed at Saint Peter. It bit at his feet and wagged its tail behind him. But the great man remained unharmed. And so, no one will direct an evil spirit toward me, no one will harm me with words, no one will curse my deeds. I have holy protection. Amen.*

You must repeat this charm three times without being distracted by anything. Then leave without looking back and observe a bloodless fast (eat no meat) for three days. You must perform this ritual every year. It cannot be held on church holidays. You may choose not to observe the fast if your health does not allow you to.

❋ Prevent Dark Entities in the Home

So that no dark entity takes up residence in your home, put mustard seeds under the carpet at the front door to your house and say:

> *He who sows, will collect. No evil will enter this house, but instead turn back and make its way to a different threshold.*

❋ Block Unclean Forces

Plant herbs and plants next to your home that will block unclean forces from entering your home. They can be lilies, marigolds, violets and cyclamen, hyssop and juniper bushes, mingled with thistle and fern. When you water them for the first time, say:

> *Green mantle, hide the people and my home from everything unclean, from everything evil.*

In addition, hang a mirror near the front door: it will repel the evil that seeks to enter your home.

❋ Amulet against Dark Power, Intent, and Words

Collect, dry, and chop mullein, lily, garlic, juniper flowers, sage, wormwood, three-color violet root, fern, and clover leaves (if you cannot get any one of these ingredients, do not worry, just use what you can find). Mix them all together and add salt to them. Pour this mixture into an old black sock and tie it with a red thread so that the herbs do not spill out. As you do so, say the following words:

> *Where you are placed, there is neither dark power, nor evil intent, nor wicked words. The salt will repel the darkness, the herbs will tear away the evil, the flowers will destroy the wicked words. No one will know, no one will pass, no one will wither, no one will die. Three times three turns, three times three twists, three times three tacks.*

Bury this protective amulet under the threshold of your front door while repeating the charm. Then no dark power will be able to enter your home.

❊ Amulet to Shield from Dark and Evil

Mix these dry herbs in equal parts: rosemary, lavender, basil, clover, mint, and laurel. Add to them a generous amount of fennel seeds, plantain seeds, garlic and marigold flowers, and violet root and speak the following charm:

> *Against dark forces, wicked words, and evil thoughts, these herbs were gathered together. Wherever they are, they will shield all from the dark and evil way by earth, and by sea, and by wind, and by fire. All that is said is as it will be, and it will never be forgotten.*

If you cannot find all of the listed herbs, then just use those that are available to you. Fill a green glass bottle or jar two-thirds full of the herbal blend and seal the jar with a stopper or lid. Place this amulet on the kitchen window. From time to time, shake the vessel and uncork it to fill your home with the fresh fragrance and protective spirit in the bottle.

❊ Spell against a Phantom Vision

If the evil force appears in your home in the form of a phantom vision, you need to mark exactly where it happened and then drive a nail into this place. You can sprinkle salt or rub garlic on the floor. As you do all of this, say:

> *Be gone from these walls, these floors, these ceilings. Shadow of disaster, go beneath the earth, fly into the skies, do not enter this house.*

❊ Protect an Object from Physical or Spell Damage

To protect a thing from possible physical or spell damage, put the object on the table. Pick up a knife with a sharp end and, envisioning that a blue flame sparks on the tip of the knife, draw an imaginary pentagram in the air above it, forming a shining star. As you do so, say the following words:

> *This is a symbol of my will and my desire, a symbol of protection*

and security in the world of man and the world of shadows from now until the end of days.

❊ Herbs and Plants against the Evil Eye

Gather and dry as many of the following herbs and plants to protect against the evil eye as you can: St. John's wort, clover, wormwood, tansy, marigold, thistle, sage, verbena, fern, juniper, hyssop, mistletoe, lily, violet root, garlic flowers, dill, laurel, clove, marjoram, rosemary, basil, and lavender. The leaves and sawdust of sandalwood, eucalyptus, patchouli, and cypress are effective as well. Mix them all together and pour the resulting herbal mixture into a small canvas pouch. As you do so, utter the following charm:

> ***Each herb is strong, each plant is wise, and together they are stronger, and together they are wiser. Together I collect them, together I conjure them, by force and daring, with wisdom to drive out evil.***

Tie this pouch with a red thread and hang it in the northern corner of your home.

❊ Reveal Who Has Cursed You

If you think that you have been cursed and suspect someone of casting it, you should perform this rite to be certain. You will need photos of those people you suspect of casting the curse, a saucer for each photo, and one needle for each photo. Arrange the photos in a semicircle near a mirror, and put a saucer with a little water in it in front of each photo. Divide up the needles into the saucers and say the following charm:

> ***I am steeping an iron needle. I want to know my offender. The one who does not sleep, does not eat, who does not feel the warmth of white light, and who holds dark thoughts against me in his heart. The one who wishes me well will be reflected in the clear iron, and the one who seeks to harm me will reveal himself in rust. Key, lock, my word, needle.***

Then cover the saucers with the photos and a large piece of black cloth. Do not touch them for seven days. After a week, remove the cloth, lift the photos, and see if any of the needles have rusted. If only one is covered in rust, it belongs to your abuser. If several are rusty, then select the rustiest one.

❊ Strong Prayer against Evil People

If you practice magic and you must protect one or more people from sorcerous influences, a special ritual will help. It is a strong prayer against evil people. To perform this rite, go to the woods during the waning moon and find an aspen. Tear off a branch and break it into the same number of pieces as there are people you want to protect. Start a small fire. Give each stick a name and burn each of them in turn with the following words:

> *Let all the malice, all the torment, all the blame, sorcery, and witchcraft burn in this fire. From now on, [name] is protected. Jesus is before him, the Mother of God is behind, and all the saints encircle him. Amen.*

When you carry out this ritual, you should wear clothes without metal components such as buttons, rivets, and the like.

❊ Protection from Bankruptcy

To protect your house from hunger and ruin, you must sacrifice to the spirits of the earth. Bury something edible near the front door; for example, a loaf of bread. (Back in time only rich people could afford to eat bread; this is why we say, "I always have bread on my table," meaning "I always have food.") As you bury your offering, say:

> *May peace and prosperity be in this house, let earthly and heavenly grace descend on it, for ever and ever. My words are strong, sure, said, and done.*

❊ Protection from Poverty

Roll a note on which you've written your request for protection into a tube and fill this tube with dry sage. Seal both ends of the tube with the wax of a green candle and wrap it with a green thread, tying it with a triple knot. While this talisman is intact and safe, you do not need to fear ruin or loss of wealth.

❊ Protection from Misfortune

If someone says that they wish you well but you suspect that they actually wish you ill, bite the tip of your tongue and think to yourself:

I wish the same to you.

❊ Protection from Someone's Schemes

To protect yourself from someone's schemes, carry a piece of green thread moistened with either your saliva or blood for a week. As you moisten the thread, say:

Everything that touches me, to the thread be transferred.

After seven days pass, make a candle (or oil lamp) with the thread as its wick. Burn the candle on a Wednesday morning. As you light it, say:

Burn, candle, bright light, quick fire. As you burn, so all dark forces will burn away.

❊ Charm against Troubles and Misfortunes

To protect yourself from the evil eye and to prevent all kinds of trouble and misfortunes, use an old key to draw three crosses on your palm. Do this just before leaving the house, but do not carry the key over your threshold, otherwise the charm will have no power.

❊ Protect Your Loved Ones

If you are afraid that something bad may happen to your loved ones, stand facing the eastern corner of your house, cross your arms in front of you, press your hands against the walls, and mentally say the names of all those you hold dear.

❊ Protect from Your Enemy's Evil Plans

Buy a small wooden box and six mirrors that are similar in size to the bottom and inside walls of the box. Glue the mirrors into the box: one mirror on the bottom, one on the lid, and the other four on the walls. Put a picture of your ill-wisher in the box (write their full name seven times on the back of it), surrounded by mirrors. Write your request for protection on a clean piece of paper and put it together with the photo inside the box. Now the enemy is ensnared in their own evil plans and cannot harm you. If you do not have a picture, write their full name on a piece of paper and place it in the mirror box. If you do not know who is seeking to hurt you, put a piece of paper with the following inscription in the box:

Let this be where all my enemies dwell.

Keep this box locked away in a secret place.

❊ Protect Food from Curses

To protect your food from secret curses (many times ill-wishers bring us hexed food to eat), use a fork and knife to draw a cross, a circle, and a pentagram over it. As you do so, say:

Dark forces be gone, wicked thoughts disappear, evil spirits vanish beneath the holy cross, the circle, and the pentagram.

❊ Bypass Wickedness and Evil

If you expect or foresee failures or misfortunes, light a yellow or orange candle and describe on a piece of paper an unwanted, but very likely, event that may or is anticipated to happen in your life. You can just write one word, such as *failure, trouble,* or *grief.* Draw a cross on top of the inscription. In doing so, you must feel that you are really removing the unwanted event from your life. Light the paper with the candle's flame and say:

With holy fire I wash away every evil, every filth, every evil thought of what was, what will be, and what should be. I will leave the left path and step onto the right path, bypass the side of wicked and evil, and control my own fate.

Collect all the remaining ash from the paper and scatter it in the wind.

❋ Talisman against Misfortune

To protect yourself from misfortune, craft a protective talisman. Write the following charm on a piece of paper:

> *I invoke the heavens. I protect myself with earth and with fire. I cleanse myself with water.*

Tie two small twigs of verbena or cypress together with a red thread so that they form a cross. As you do this, read the charm you wrote. Fold the paper and sew it and the cross into a small leather bag that you carry around your neck or close to your heart.

❋ Protect against the Misfortune from a Broken Mirror

If the bad luck caused by a broken mirror has already affected you, do the following: Place a short gray candle in an old iron pan. This candle represents your problems or misfortunes. Pour an infusion of yarrow into the bowl and light the candle. When the candle burns down to the infusion and the wick is extinguished, your problem will be eliminated. Then, pour out the infusion and bury the candle along with the pot in black earth.

❋ Sacrifice an Apple to Resolve Your Problems

Your problems will disappear if you do the following: Hold a large ripe apple between your palms. Imagine all your difficulties and troubles going into this fruit. Then cut the apple into four pieces and bury them in the ground in different places. As you do so, you must understand that you are sacrificing to the forces of nature and that these forces will contribute to the successful resolution of your concerns.

❋ Relieve Your Worries

When you are plagued by any intense stress, worries, problems, or failures, speak all your troubled thoughts aloud while holding an empty bottle to your lips. When you finish talking, immediately seal the bottle. Take it to a deserted place and bury it in the ground. Rest assured that you have forever buried all your troubles.

PROTECTION ON THE ROAD

❊ A Road Talisman against Danger

Make a pouch out of blue fabric. Put a white feather, an old key, and a small carnation into it. Tie up the pouch with a ribbon of the same color and say:

> *In the fields, on the road, in the desert, and on the sea protect me from unkind people, keep me safe from accident or injury, clear the clouds from the sky, do not allow storms or blizzards along the way, on the road, in the morning, in the afternoon, in the evening, and at night.*

Take this talisman with you on the road, and you will be free of fatigue and safe from danger.

❊ A Road Amulet for Protection

A road amulet is made like this: Cut 2 inches from the thickest branch of an elderberry bush and remove the soft core. Mix equal parts powdered horse hoof, spiderweb, hair of a wild dog, and withered snake skin (if it is difficult for you to get all these components, then use dried and powdered plantain soaked in your sweat). Insert the charm material into the hole you created in the piece of branch. Seal the branch on both ends with small plugs cut out of ash. On the distant road, put this amulet in your travel bag and you will be protected from wild beasts, venomous spiders, snakes, and sly people. You will not be concerned about fatigue, you will not lose your footing, and you will always be fresh and healthy.

❊ Button Spell to Protect a Traveler

To avoid trouble on the road and safely return home from a trip, the day before departure for a long trip, go to five different roads and take a small pebble from each of them. Place four of them next to your house at the corners of the building and throw the fifth in front of the threshold. Read the following charm over a button:

> *By my deeds and by my word, [name of the traveler] will travel with determination, day and night, morning and evening, until he returns.*

Next, sew this button to the clothing of the person who is going on the trip.

❋ Road Protection: Key and Coin to Be Left at Home

Before you go on a long journey, draw three crosses on your left palm with the tip of a key. Draw three crosses on your right palm, but with a coin, not a key. Do not take the key or the coin with you on your trip. Leave them at home so that you do not encounter trouble on the way and return safely.

❋ Road Protection for Self or Loved Ones

To protect yourself or one of your loved ones on the road, light a candle and sprinkle a powder made of dried plantain leaves over it. At the same time, read the following charm:

> *On his journey, the road will be straight for [name]. On his journey, evil and sly people will not be able to find [name]. On his journey, he will not lose his footing, his hands will not be harmed, and his head will be protected. He will not get lost in a foreign land and will return to his beloved home.*

❋ Charm on a Plantain Leaf

When you go on a trip, tear off a plantain leaf and say the following charm:

> *The road at my face, my back to the gate, my head to the sky, and the world on all sides. My path leads from field to field, from meadow to meadow, to far-off lands. In those fields and meadows and all along my path are plentiful herbs. Plentiful herbs that overpower the evil and the sly so that the wicked do not affect me with their evil thoughts, do not accomplish dark deeds against me, do not steal my possessions, do not curse me. They are overwhelmed by herbs, overcome by me.*

The mountains are high, the valleys are broad, the rivers are deep, the forests are dark, the roads are straight, the ways roundabout so that I do not lose my footing, calluses cannot form, I will catch no colds, I will not be led astray, my heart will not break. All that I say is as it will be.

Put this leaf in your pocket or in your travel bag and safely start your journey.

❊ Belt of Swiftness Amulet

If your trip requires you to spend much of your time traveling on foot, make a special amulet called a belt of swiftness. To do this, cut one strip each of red fabric and white fabric, long enough to tie around your ankle. Place them together, with three horsehairs taken from the mane of a young stallion between them. Sew the strips together, saying:

Along roundabout routes, by leaps and bounds on the path and where the paths meet, on the road and where the roads meet, my feet will not waver, will not lose time. The one who sews the belt, who utters the charm will always be swift and tireless.

Before you depart, tie the amulet you made around your left ankle with the white side inward and say:

With this secret object, luck and ease will be in my path day and night.

❊ Another Belt of Swiftness Method

Gather and dry red wormwood. Sew the wormwood into a strip of rabbit's skin as you speak the charm:

You will not get lost on the road nor will you get lost in snowstorms. You will not stray from the path nor stumble in the mud. You will avoid the black forest of the beast and avoid all those who are evil and sly. You will not lose your footing, nor hurt your hands, nor catch a chill. You will find yourself in the right place at the right time. My words will prove right and true in day and night; under the bright moon and under the new moon; under the bright sun, at dawn, and at sunset.

Keep this amulet with you always, and you will never tire. Your path will always be easy and safe.

SPELLS TO REMOVE THE EVIL EYE AND CURSES

❊ Getting Rid of the Evil Eye and Curses

To remove any damage caused by the evil eye and protect against the evil eye, go to three different wells before sunrise and pour water from each of them into three buckets (it might be a challenge to find three wells, but you should do so because well water is necessary for this type of old world conjuring). As you return home, put an empty bucket in the center of your house, light four candles placed around it, and put two long knives on top of it in the shape of a cross. Pour water from the three buckets into the empty bucket through the crossed knives and at the same time say:

Three waters, three sisters, three baptizers. Two swords, two brothers. Only faith stands alone. The first water will cleanse the soul; the second water will heal the heart; the third water will illuminate the thoughts. All evil spirits and fears will be exterminated; faith will confirm the truth of belief.

Once you have done this, remove the knives from the bucket and pour the spelled water over your head.

❊ Escape Love Sorcery

To neutralize love sorcery, perform one simple but very effective action. Go to some quiet and unpopulated place, where no one can bother you, and dig a small hole. Hold about four or five sewing needles in each hand. Concentrate and imagine that all sorcery-influenced feelings have moved into the needles. Open your hands and throw all the needles into the pit with a sharp movement. Bury them and put a lighted candle on top. Leave it to burn out, then go back home.

❋ Wash Away Sorrow

Collect wild heather before sunrise, place it in boiling water, and, when the water cools down a little, wash your face, chest, and hands in it. As you do so, say the following charm:

Mother rapid water, wash and take away all the fright and bite, all the sorrow and pain, all the sick and the injured.

Afterward, collect the dirty water that remains and pour it down the drain.

❋ Mirrors to Reflect Curses Away from Your Children

At midnight, arrange two small mirrors so that they are reflected in one another. Stand between them holding a candle and recite forty times:

Dark night, each mirror reflects the other. Reflect, as well, the spell from me, the enemy's curse, the mark of hell. I ask forty times that you may hear my plea. May you ward away this curse, this hex, this enchantment from me and mine [name of your son or daughter]. Amen.

Once that is done, cleanse yourself in well water or water from a holy spring and use that same water to cleanse your children. Pour out the remaining water under a tree.

❋ Remove Dark Forces Using Water, Coals, and Salt

Pour a glass of pure springwater and put in three coals and three pinches of salt. Whisper over this water the following secret words:

Holy water will purify, charcoal will cleanse, and salt will sanitize dark forces, evil thoughts, and all wicked things.

Discreetly sprinkle this water on the cursed one and say:

Be gone all torment, be gone all evil, from [name] to dark forests, to dry trees, to decaying logs, to marshy swamps, to places where people do not walk, beasts do not wander, birds do not fly, where there is only the inhuman forest spirit sitting in the hollow.

❋ Remove Dark Forces Using Water

Pour a bowl of pure springwater. Go to your door and do this: Three times, pour a spoonful of water from the bowl over the door handle. Then go to another door and repeat those steps. Do the same with all door handles throughout the house. The person cursed by sorcery should not see what you are doing. When you have finished, approach the cursed person and quickly splash them with water, saying:

> *Go, through the door and past the porch, go, through the spelled water. All evil, be gone, all torment from [name].*

After you do so, have them drink three sips of the water.

❋ Remove Curses Using Wax

Put wax in a deep bowl and melt it, placing the bowl over a fire. Sit a cursed person on a stool facing east. Cover him with a white towel. Hold a bowl of pure springwater over him and pour melted wax into it. As you do so, read the following charm:

> *I spell [name] from illness, torment, labor, and fatigue, from gray eye, from black eye, from the warlock, from the witch. Be gone from [name] all the ills, bruises, and pinpricks born and fated for dark forests, to dry trees where people do not walk, where cattle do not wander, where birds do not fly, where beasts do not roam.*

When you have finished the spell, discard all the wax and pour the water into a river. Repeat these steps the next day in the morning and again in the evening. If the curse was very strong, repeat it three more times.

❋ Remove a Curse Using Your Hands

Stand behind a cursed person, put your hands on their shoulders, and say:

> *There are three small rays of light on you: one is clear, one is red, the third is [the name of the cursed].*

After that, put your hands on the accursed one's back and, without lifting your hands, drag them all the way down to the ankles. At the same time, say:

> *As the clear ray shines, as the red fades away, so all injuries and ailments will go away with the third [name].*

Now, envision that along with the movement of your hands along the cursed person's body, all the affliction and misfortune is draining, descending, and disappearing into the earth. When you have completed the movement, shake your hands. Repeat the charm and all the other steps two more times. After finishing the charm, do not forget to wash your hands in running water.

❋ Remove the Evil Eye Using Salt, Ash, and Coal

Throw three pinches of salt, three pinches of ash, and three small coals into a container of water. Spray the water on someone afflicted by the evil eye and read the following charm:

> *Salty salt, bitter ash, black coal. With salt I will cleanse evil, with ash incinerate all dark spirits, with coal eradicate the blackness. Whoever consumes the salt, all their fear and pain will fall away; whoever consumes the ashes, all their ailments and diseases will be flushed out; whoever consumes the coal, all their curses and struggles will fly away.*

Then have the cursed one drink some of the water.

❋ Lift a Curse Using a Padlock

To lift the curse, lock an old padlock while you are dragging it or passing it over your body from your head to your toes—you must go from up down, not the opposite—and say the charm:

> *I close this lock against all the ways, all the paths for the whips and pains of [name of the cursed person], so that it will have no access of any kind. Not in day nor at night, nor at dawn, nor at dusk, nor at the new moon, nor at the full moon, nor with a*

> ***clear sun, nor with a dark cloud, nor with wind, nor with rain, nor with drought, nor with water. Return from whence you came. Do not take a detour, nor a side path, but go in the very opposite direction. These words are my lock and key from now until the end of time.***

Throw away the padlock in the middle of a river or bury it in the ground in a place where no one will find it.

❋ Lift a Curse Using Dry Pine

Find a dry branch that fell from a pine tree and wave it around the head, abdomen, and knees of the cursed person, uttering the charm:

> ***As the pine trees dried and the twigs and branches withered, all the struggles and pains of [name] will dry up and wither. They flee from his head, they fall away from his stomach, flee from the knees, flee for dry land.***

After completing this spell, bury the branch deep in the ground.

❋ Potion to Lift a Curse

Give the cursed one a special potion. Gather sage at the last quarter of the moon, bay leaf at the new moon, marjoram at the first quarter of the moon, and dill at the full moon. When the moon sets, boil a glass of red wine and, uttering the charm, throw three pinches of each herb into it. The charm sounds like this:

> ***Cursed thrice, thrice charmed, at once freed and cursed. The one who drinks will live a healthy life when morning comes. The one who sowed the curse will not reap anything from him.***

When the wine cools, it must be strained before being consumed by the cursed person.

❋ Lift the Evil Eye Using Nettle

To lift the evil eye, put a little nettle on a small plate, sprinkle it with alcohol, and set it on fire. When the fire goes out and the seed starts to smoke, smudge the afflicted one with it so that the smoke gets into their eyes. At the same time, say the following words:

> *As neither water nor dew can hold a gray duck, so too can [name] hold no struggles, no suffering, no numbness, no pain.*

You can say another charm for even more effectiveness:

> *Through a clean tear, through white dew, all the suffering, struggles, the evil gaze and bite fall away from [name]. They flee to the black earth, to the marshy swamps, to dense forests, where people do not walk, where cattle do not wander, where beasts do not prowl. All my words are spelled, enchanted, and it will be so.*

❊ Remove a Curse from a Child

A child's curse should be removed as follows: Take a long red thread and tie a knot at one end of it. Measure the child's height with this thread and mark it with a second knot. Then, with the child's hands outstretched to the sides, attach the second knot to the right middle finger and the free end to the left middle finger. Mark the length with a third knot and say:

> *With three knots marked, with secret words healed.*

After doing this, drill a small hole in a doorway and completely insert this thread into it. Drive a wooden cork or a dry branch into the hole and say:

> *As this sealed side of the door cannot be opened, so [name] is no longer open to the turmoil that will forever remain in this hole.*

❊ Remove a Curse of Male Impotence

To remove a curse of male impotence, pour springwater into a mug, put a penny in it, and read the following charm over the water:

> *I'll rise at dawn, I'll wash myself in dew, I'll go out the door, through the gate, and into an open field. And in the open field*

there will be a copper oak, an oak that the wind does not bend, storms do not break. So will [name] stand before a female, neither bending at the hollow place nor breaking at the hollow place. He will stand better than he once did, straighter than before, firmer than solid, stronger than strong. By my words, this is the key and the lock, now and forever.

Then let the cursed man drink the spelled water.

❊ Get Rid of All Evil

To get rid of all evil, go to a sparsely populated place; for example, an open field or a forest. Find a large flat stone. Set two white candles on it. Place a glass of pure springwater between them. Kneel before the altar. Hold your hands over the glass and envision that all the dark power, all the problems and misfortunes, flow into the water in the glass. As you do so, repeat the following charm:

Clear water, clear fire, black earth, remove everything dark, multiply everything light.

Then topple the glass so that all the water spills onto the stone and the glass falls to the black earth. Blow out the candles, leave them with the lass on the stone, and return home. On the way back, do not say a word to anyone and do not talk at all.

❊ Remove a Curse from Your Home

When you find evidence of curse work in your house, such as threaded bones or feathers, black wool with needles, a bag of ashes, or just a sheet of paper with curses written on it, take it in your right hand, go to the open door, stand with the threshold at your back, and say:

Misfortune, you've lived in this house. Now live in another place, and take everything with you!

Throw away what you are holding, over your left shoulder, past the threshold, and finish the charm:

What is behind me will not come back!

Next, you will need to clear your home from curses. To do this, take the discarded magical items to a deserted place and, depending on what materials were used for the curse, burn or tear a piece of paper with curses written on it, scatter ashes in the wind, untangle a hank of wool, or untie the thread connecting feathers and scatter the feathers in different directions. As you do so, say:

Whoever did this dark work, your darkness returns to you!
Whoever had wicked thoughts, your thoughts return to you!
Whoever committed evil, you have committed this evil upon yourself! It crawls on the ground, swims in the water, burns in the fire, scatters in the wind along the same road, along the same path, toward the same fate, the same way. What remains will not reach its target, and all that was or could be will only go toward the person who did this evil, for he has sinned against good people!

Having done this, return home in a roundabout way.

❊ Remove a House Curse Using a Broom

If, when you leave the house, you find some clear signs of black sorcery near your doorstep, such as melted candles, ashes, needles, scattered poppy seeds or black pepper, yellow sulfur, or the most common, salt, do the following: Take a broom in your left hand, stand with your back to the threshold, and, taking a step back, step over and through the scattered salt, needles, and other magical objects. Then put your left hand with the broom behind your back. Keep your right hand in front of your face. Bow at the waist in this position toward the ground, take a pinch of the salt or other object lying at your doorstep, and say:

Hello, misfortune. I opened the gate, but you will not enter my house.

Straighten up, throw the object over your left shoulder, and finish the charm:

It's clear I do not wish for you.

All this must be done with the door open. Now, slam it. Get rid of all that lies before your doorstep by collecting all the rubbish in a paper bag with a broom. After that, go to a deserted place and leave all the garbage there, along with the broom.

SPELLS TO STOP GOSSIP AND SCHEMING

❋ Prevent the Spread of False Rumors

To prevent others from spreading false rumors, cut a circle out of paper and write the name of the person slandering your name on it. Put this circle in the bottom of a cup (the size of the circle must match the dimensions of the bottom of the cup). Set an ice cube on top of the paper circle. Then break an egg and pour both the yolk and the white over the ice and onto the circle. Put the cup with all its contents in an icy place.

❋ Muffle Someone's Lies

If someone is gossiping about you, put white flower petals into a small wooden or cardboard box. Light a red candle and burn a photo of the lying person or a piece of paper with their full name written on it. As you do so, say:

> *Now all your lies are muffled. Only truth and honesty will be in your language and in your words.*

Throw the ashes into the box with the petals, mix it all, and store it for three days in a secret place. Then go out into an open field, scatter the petals and ashes to the wind, and repeat the charm.

❋ Stop Someone Who's Spreading Rumors, Using Thread

If you know exactly who is spreading false rumors about you, and you have a picture of them, thread gray thread into a needle and sew it onto the picture over your enemy's mouth.

❋ Stop Someone Who's Spreading Rumors, Using a Padlock

When a person you know is spreading false rumors about you, put a closed padlock and three bay leaves into a pouch made of blue cloth. Either throw the pouch away near their house or bury it near them. Keep the key to the lock at your house.

❋ Stop Someone Who's Spreading Rumors, Using a Bottle and Wax

When you need to eliminate unwanted gossip and nullify the efforts of a person who is trying to hurt you, write the name of your ill-wisher on a sheet of paper (better yet, use a photo of the person with their full name written seven times on the back of it). Roll the paper into a tube, tie it with a red thread, and put it in a bottle made of dark glass. Mix sea salt, oak moss, magnetic metal shavings, and plantain seeds in a bowl. Fill the bottle almost to the top with this mixture and seal it with a wax stopper. This is done by dripping molten red candle wax directly into the neck until it completely closes the hole. Bury this bottle in a deserted place, and while it is secret and safe, your enemy will not be able to harm you.

❋ Amulet to Stop an Envious Person Who Maligns You

To pay back those who speak ill about you through envy, get a red rose and set a small glass vessel on a table in front of you. Cut off all the rose thorns and throw them into the vessel one by one, saying the same words every time:

> *Each thorn for each evil tongue, for each injustice.*

Then tear off all the rose petals and place them one by one in the vessel with the thorns. This time say:

> *Lay softly, sleep tight, think about yourself, forget about everyone else; everything is as it should be.*

Pour saltwater in with the petals and thorns, seal the jar with a stopper, wrap it in a dark cloth, and tie it with a red thread knotted nine times. If you know who your ill-wisher is, hide the amulet in their home or leave it at their door. If you do not know who is performing the evil deeds, bury the vessel in the ground near your house so that it protects you from future accusations and slander.

❋ Spell to Neutralize the Ability of Lies to Harm You

If you think that someone is lying to you, concocting schemes against you, or spreading gossip about you, write their name on a sheet of paper nine times and then cross out each one. Put the paper on a table and place a red candle on it. Burn the candle for seven days, imagining as you do that all the hate, anger, or lying that was hidden from you falling apart, losing the ability to harm you and damage you.

SPELLS TO CURSE AND PUNISH YOUR ENEMIES

❋ Curse Your Enemy

Take out a piece of clothing and a strand of your enemy's hair. Cut the cloth into thin strips to get nine pieces of thread. Light two black candles. Put these nine threads together and read the following charm:

> *Nine fields are clean, three trees are withered, swamps are hot, deep pools, I myself call the devil; yes, make a firm loop, let me have the power of your rule over your hellish slaves, and as you rule those souls so from this moment will I take the soul and body of [name of the enemy] to rule them, [enemy's name] is mine, [your name]. In the noose [enemy's name], let me and not the hanging man lead them, like a dog tethered to a chain. Amen.*

Weave the nine threads into one and add your enemy's hair into it. As you weave, say the following charm:

> *I invoke the Nine Forces of the Underworld,*
> *Through these forces, [enemy's name] will submit to me, [your name].*

From the world of the whole [enemy's name] I take,
In a word, the secret [enemy's name] is closed.
The power of black on the heels of [enemy's name] I put,
Before you [enemy's name] I call,
Back to him to obey.
I deprive [enemy's name] of the will with the hellish seal,
In [enemy's name] there is no thought,
And turn to [enemy's name]'s deeds.
Crawl, indulge,
For me, [your name], [enemy's name] will pray.
He will not search for an escape.
Or else [enemy's name] will enter his own grave.
So through the thread, the body, spirit, soul of [enemy's name],
in my name, [your name], is transformed.
With a devilish curse, a demonic curse, you, [enemy's name],
have the will to fulfill all that I, [your name], wish.
And if you do not perform,
That the devil himself will drive you.
Amen.

When the thread is woven, tie one end of it to make a loop. When you tie the loop, say:

The devil came by a noose, but left by the door,
Yes, [name] began to seek,
And as he found, so conjured he [name] became.
The seal of his forehead was singed,
In me, [your name], [enemy's name]
Not a word, but a deed he drew.
So now [enemy's name] will come to me, [your name],
In service, for thirteen years serving.
Let your body, [enemy's name], submit,
Let your soul, [enemy's name], be softer than beeswax.
So if I die, [enemy's name], I command you,
That life will be taken away from you.
So listen, [enemy's name], to me, [your name],

By my will, [your name],
You are [enemy's name] in the morning and in the evening.
So be it,
And [enemy's name] belongs to me, [your name], until I die.
Amen.

Store the loop in a secret place. You will exert full power over the person to whom it is done.

❈ Curse to Be Done on Tuesday or Saturday

Perform this curse during a full moon or a waning moon, on a Tuesday or Saturday.

You will need two mirrors of the same size, a black candle, and black thread. Light a candle, put a photo of the person to be cursed between the mirrors (place the photo between the mirror surfaces), and start tying the mirrors crosswise. As you do so, read the following charm three times:

In the name of the hearer, by the power of the punisher, by the blackness of the black, by the power of the dark, you, my enemy, [name], be gone from me, leave, turn away, turn from body into shadow, dissolve, dissolve, dissolve . . .
I'll cover you with a shroud of black, the force of my charm,
Do not breathe, do not exhale, you cannot escape from captivity, there is no freedom for you, [name].
I curse you with a black curse, a triadic spell, a filthy fate, beastly bondage.
It is not possible for you, my enemy, to live, but you will wander in shadow.
You are entangled in the web of black, I envelop you with hellfire,
I will deafen, I will blind, I will kill, I will destroy your fate.
From the white world I seal you away, in a glass coffin, with a black candle, as I sing!
It is said, done, molded, finished, and no begging, no sorcerer, no healer, no sorceress will come to your aid. So be it!

After you read the charm, tie a knot, seal it with black candle wax. Hide the mirrors in the northern corner of the room for nine days, and afterward, bury it under a cemetery fence with the appropriate offering left at the cemetery crossroad.

❋ Close the Roads for Someone

Take thirteen nails and drive them into the pathway leading to the person you want to curse by saying:

> *Nails into your feet, there is no path to you, no roads! So be it!*

❋ Punish Enemies and Ill-Wishers

If someone is envious of you, harbors vicious plans against you, or has already committed some injustice toward you, write their full name on a sheet of paper and, if you know it, their date of birth. Look at this paper and imagine the face of your ill-wisher. Then pour water into a small jar. Roll the paper into a tube, tie it with a black thread, and throw it into the water. Put the jar of water in an icy place to freeze and say:

> *With the eyes of a dragon and the wings of an angel, I spell the one against me so that he will not find his way in the world.*

Once you have done this, rest assured that the ice formed in the jar will safely hold back the evil thoughts and actions of the person who wishes you ill.

❋ Make Ill-Wishers Leave You Alone Forever

This charm is used to make the ill-wishers leave you alone forever. It will help if you know who has unfriendly feelings toward you. Wait for the moment when the evil-doer is passing by you and read the following words while staring at their back:

> *I shoot this sharp arrow. It pierces through him without touching his face, nor his eyes, nor his eyebrows. It will fly right into his heart. It will lash, slash, and gash my enemy, [name]; cause him the same suffering that I had to experience; and make him unhappy until his heart is healed. Amen.*

❋ Sorcery for Irreparable Evil

If an irreparable evil that cannot be forgiven has been inflicted on you, perform counter-sorcery. Take two needles. One should be thick and long, the other short and thin. Insert the smaller needle into the larger needle's eye. Tie the place where the needles are connected with a black thread so that they hold tightly together and say:

> *Your needle is long, mine short, yours is evil, mine is goodness.*
> *I pierce your evil, I return everything that you inflicted on me,*
> *everything that have you done to me, everything that I received,*
> *back now, this very moment, for forever and ever!*

Insert the large needle into the door or the doorframe of your ill-wisher's house so that your short needle is pointing to the right. Repeat the previous charm.

❋ Punish Someone Who Has Offended You

To punish a person who has offended you, you will need some of their hair. Fold the hair in a white cloth, put it on a table, and, striking the cloth with a stick, speak the following charm:

> *As this hair now receives blows and pain, so its master will receive blows and pain.*

This sorcery should be used only when you are dealt a truly mortal offense or have been hurt by an irreparable evil.

❋ Spell to Make Ill-Wishers Lose Their Power

Pour clean springwater into a glass jar. Place a mirror on a table, put the Bible in front of it, and put the jar of water on it. Put a candle between the book and the mirror. Sit at the table and look into the mirror through the water. Say:

> *He who is good will remain good, he who is evil will be dealt evil,*
> *and he who utters unholy words will choke on those words.*

Go to a deserted place and sprinkle the water in four directions. If you know your ill-wisher, pour the water out at their house. All their plans will lose their power, and the evil they do will turn against them.

❋ Return a Curse to the One Who Sent It

To return a curse sent to you to the one who created it, perform counter-sorcery. Take the liver or heart of some animal or bird, put a photo of the offender on top of it, and stick nine sharp little sticks or needles into it. As you insert the first needle, say:

This is the person who wronged me!

The second needle should pierce the heart or liver at the moment you say:

This is the person who cursed me!

Insert the third needle with the words:

This is the person who hurts me with his dark envy.

The fourth:

This needle will pierce his heart (liver)!

The fifth:

This needle will pierce his tongue!

The sixth:

This needle will tame his wicked thoughts!

The seventh:

All his strength will leave him!

The eighth:

His spirit will die!

Finally, insert the ninth and last needle, saying:

Black eye, return to your maker!

After that, wrap the heart or liver in a linen cloth and bury it in a manure pit or hide it near your enemy's home.

❊ Punish Your Enemies Using Sticks and Salt

If you want to severely punish your enemies or those who hurt you, the next ritual will help you to do so. Cut a few twigs (as many as you have enemies) from an apple tree or any other deciduous tree. Cut each stick smoothly on both ends so that they measure 1.5–2 inches. Cut away one side on each stick to get a flat surface. Then write the name of your offender in pencil on that cleared side. Afterward, put these sticks in a glass jar and fill it with sea salt, while saying the following charm:

> *[Name], [name] . . . Let your hearts dry, unworthy as you are.*
> *Amen.*

Close the lid and store the jar for at least seven days in a dark place. Once seven days have passed, the jar's contents should be thrown away outside.

❊ Powerful Rite to Wither an Enemy

This is very powerful rite. Before you use it, think carefully about whether it is worth taking sin on your soul. Plant a small pot with a hot chili pepper. Call this pepper the name of your enemy or rival, take care of it, water it regularly, talk to it (politely). Write the name of your enemy on a scrap of red cloth and tie it to the pepper plant when it starts to bloom. Then as soon as the first small fruits appear, stop watering it and begin to say the following charm to it three times a day:

> *For your deceitful deeds, [name], you will wither inside and out.*
> *Amen.*

The person with whom you associate this plant will really begin to wither away. To save that person, you must remove the red scrap of cloth from the pepper plant before it dies.

❋ Curse Your Enemy Using Mirror and Thread

You will need a mirror, black thread, and a photo of your enemy. The photo and mirror should be about the same size. Do this at midnight: Put the photo on the mirror and wrap them together with the black thread crosswise. Go to a crossroads and throw the mirror with all your might to break it while saying:

> *The mirror is broken, it does not concern me,*
> *And so the fate of [name of the enemy] is broken.*
> *As this mirror will not become a whole, so will [name of the enemy] have no happiness.*
> *So be it!*

Go home without looking back and without talking to anyone.

6

House and Home Spells

Our home is our protection and our shelter. We believe that there is a house spirit that lives in a home. It is an energy that helps us, strengthens, heals, and protects. This energy can leave a home if there is no order and peace in it. Some people can also bring, intentionally or unintentionally, chaos and negative energy into their home, which will destroy the home spirit or make the spirit leave or become aggressive. To prevent this from happening, it is necessary from time to time to clean the energy of our home, read prayers and spells that protect the house, and conduct rituals that help to saturate the space with protective energy and positivity.

SPELLS FOR MOVING TO A NEW HOUSE

❊ Before Moving to a New House

Before you leave home for good and move to a new place, take ash from the stove or dust and dirt swept off the floor and put it into a small bottle. Walk around the house with this bottle three times. As you do, repeat the following charm:

> *Ashes to ashes, dust to dust, all that is mine to me. I will live in a new place. I will not grieve about my old home. I will bring along*

all that is good and right. I will find happiness and prosperity in a new place.

After you have done this, seal the bottle with a stopper. Take this bottle to a deserted place and bury it deep in the ground.

❋ On the Eve of Moving

On the eve of moving you must knead dough in your old home. The next day, take it to your new home and bake bread there. Wait three days to eat this bread, then buy a lot of food and drink. Set your dining room table with a place for each person who will live in the new house, plus one more for the spirit of the house. Feed each member of the household a piece of the bread. Salt one slice heavily, stick a coin in it facing upward, and hide it behind the stove (or the oven). After that, bow to the stove three times, approaching it from three different sides, and say:

Master, father, spirit behind the stove, take my food, my bread, and salt. Love my family, bring happiness and success and luck, and preserve our home.

❋ Call a House Spirit

To call a house spirit to join you in a new house, it is necessary to put an old boot or an old shoe in every corner of the old house. As you do so, you should bow and say:

Master, father, let's go to a new house to live, to be, and to prosper.

Then you must take the boot to the new dwelling, put it in a closet, and say:

Master, father, this is your new home. Live in it for your joy and ours.

You should not bring a broom from your old home, but if you decide to bring one with you to the new dwelling, bring it into the house through the window, not the door.

❋ Spell to See the House Spirit

On the first day of November, you will be able to see the house spirit. Near midnight, take a black candle and a fresh egg from a speckled hen and go to a barn. Stand at the front door, but do not enter. Hold the egg in your left hand, light the candle in your right hand, and say:

> *Master of the household, master of the house, come to me not as a dog, nor as a cat, but as I am. I come with an offering.*

Repeat these words until the spirit appears in human form. Then put the egg on the threshold and run into your house without looking back. Do this to indulge and appease the spirit so that he protects the household.

SPELLS FOR PEACE AND TRANQUILLITY IN THE HOUSE

❋ Talisman for Peace and Tranquillity in the House

To preserve peace and tranquillity in your home, crush resin or pitch in a mortar or small bowl and add equal parts salt and granulated sugar. Fill a small bottle with this mixture and seal it with a stopper. Keep this talisman in the kitchen. If you cannot get pitch, use spruce or pine needles instead.

❋ Spell to Unite Your Family

To unite your family, cut human shapes out of paper. Cut out as many as there are people in your family. Write the name of one household member on each paper figure, coat them in honey, and place them together so that they stick to one other. Put the figures into an envelope, seal it, and keep it secret and safe.

❋ Spell to Ensure Reconciliation

To ensure reconciliation between household members and avoid new family scandals and arguments, use a white rose to sprinkle holy water in all the rooms of your house. Dip the rosebud into the liquid and, holding it by the stem, sprinkle water in three directions: in front of you, to your left, and to your right.

❋ Spell to Avoid Trouble in the Home

If there is trouble in your home or you sense it coming, put a silver coin for each year you have lived with your husband or wife into a glass filled with water and a gold one for each year you plan to live with him or her. Say the following charm over the water:

> *With gold and silver, past and future, I conjure you, the Power of Water, to preserve and multiply, to preserve and maintain peace and harmony, purity and faithfulness from this day forth.*

Sprinkle this water on your spouse and wash your face and hands with it.

❋ Spell to Remove Strife and Conflict

If there is constant strife and conflict in your house, then do the following: Tear seven twigs from a rowan tree. They should be no more than 4 inches long. Fashion a whisk by tying them all together with green thread. When you come home, pour pure springwater into a pot, put it on the stove, and bring it to a boil. Throw three pinches of powdered thistle or juniper into the boiling water and say three times:

> *Let this water be imbued with purity, faith, and sanctity.*

After a while, remove the pot from the stove. When the infusion has cooled, take the pot in your hands and sprinkle the water on the floor in every room of your house with the rowan whisk. As you do so, say:

> *With holy water, secret words, and sorcery, I cleanse the walls, ceiling, and floors of all evil spirits, of all wickedness and unbelief. May there be peace in this house, grace under this roof, peace and prosperity within these walls, prosperity and plenty behind these curtains.*

When you have completed this spell, pour the rest of the water outside at the front door. Do not discard the rowan whisk: keep it in a secluded place as a protective talisman against the forces of evil and unbelief.

❋ Spell to Remove a Curse on the Home

If the scandals and conflicts in your home have been caused by a curse, then light a candle and hold it as you walk around the room. First, go from one corner to the opposite corner (diagonally), then turn right and walk along the wall to the next corner, and walk diagonally to the opposite corner again. When you pass through the center of the room, stop and draw a cross in the space in front of you with the candle, uttering the following words:

To cleanse with sacred fire.

As you near each corner, do the same. You must pass through the center of the room exactly eight times and go to each corner three times. When you have finished, get a bowl of holy water and walk the same path you did before. This time, when you stop in the center of the room and in the corners, sprinkle the space in front of you with water and say:

To clear with holy water.

Next, replace the water with salt, which you must scatter in the same places while saying:

To expel with the salt of the earth.

❋ Spell to Exterminate Evil

Put an old and out-of-use iron pot on the stove, fill it two-thirds of the way with cold water and throw in three pinches of thistles, a pinch of rosemary, and a pinch of coarse salt. Next, tie together two dirty kitchen towels. When your potion begins to boil, dip these towels into it and say:

The first to the first, the second to the second, and the third to the third. Gather all evil spirits and dark power into one circle, exterminate it, drive it away from the young and the old. It has no place in this house, nor a half-place. It has no life, no existence, only torment and starvation.

After a while, remove the pot from the heat and allow the water to cool completely. Then go to a deserted area, bury the towels deep in the ground, pour the rest of the water around it, and say:

As I place these rags in the earth, all wickedness and evil will be trapped where they are tied and never return.

On your way home, leave the pot at the crossroad of two footpaths or throw it in someone else's yard.

❋ Spell to Banish Evil and Wickedness

Ask all those who live in your house to leave and only start your spell work after they are gone. Pour water into a kettle and put it on the stove. When the water boils, throw three pinches of valerian root, three pinches of astragalus root, and three pinches of powdered thistle into it. Say the following charm:

> *I unite these three herbs; I unite them against evil and wickedness.*

Open all the doors and windows in the house, remove the kettle from the stove, and take it to the room farthest away from the kitchen. Scald the threshold of this room with boiling water and say:

> *With this charm, I call you, with this boiling water I command you! Be gone from this threshold, all evil spirits, all dark and wicked forces! Do not hide in the corners, do not flee into the other rooms, but go directly to the exit!*

Then go to the next room, pour the water over its threshold, and repeat the charm. You must pour boiling water on all the thresholds in your house. Do not forget to repeat the spell. The threshold of the front door must be scalded last. When doing so, say the following words:

> *Be gone from this house, all evil spirits, all dark and wicked forces! Do not crawl, do not walk, but run! Do not walk, do not run, but swim! Do not run, do not swim, but fly straight to the depths of hell, straight into the black pit!*

❋ Devil Be Gone

Prepare an infusion of thistle or juniper in saltwater. Sprinkle this infusion in the corners and on the walls of the house while reading the following charm:

> *Oh, black, cock-eyed, barefoot devil, be gone from this house,*
> *from the doors and all four corners, from the roof and the walls,*

from the floor and the earth! Here you will receive no praise, no sympathy, no place, no rest, but only aches and pains, torment and sickness. You have your house and station on a barren mountain, in a black cave, in a deep river in the yawning earth. Return to your house and do not touch, nor trample, nor harm anyone! Live in your own home and forget this place. As the rain falls, so my enemy will leave. As the snow falls, so the evil devil will fall asleep. And so it shall be, forever and ever!

Once you perform this magical cleansing, open wide all the windows and doors so that all evil forces can easily leave your home.

SPELLS TO GET RID OF HOUSEHOLD VERMIN

❋ Get Rid of Mice and Rats

To get rid of mice and rats, prepare a steeped broth of verbena. Sprinkle it liberally around the house and repeat the following charm:

Be gone from this house, everything that creeps, everything that crawls, everything gray, white, black, or any other mouselike color.

❋ Get Rid of Mice and Cockroaches

Make from wax the figure of a mouse, pierce it with a pin, and say:

So shall it be with all of your kind if you do not go to another master.

Put this figure where you last saw the mouse.

To drive out cockroaches living in your home, put a round mirror at the bottom of a glass jar. Catch one of the cockroaches and put it into the jar. Keep it there for a while, then say the following charm:

Go directly to someone else's home and take your brothers with you. Do not come back again, or else all your kind will be destroyed with hot water, swift fire, and spells from my own lips.

Then set the cockroach free.

❊ Expel Cockroaches

To expel cockroaches or prevent them from appearing, pour water into a small cup and add a few drops of eucalyptus oil. Sprinkle it into all the corners of the house and say:

> *There are not now nor will there be cockroaches here; their black and red hordes have come and gone. There is no place for their kind here and never will be. So it was and so it shall be.*

You can also place dried eucalyptus leaves in the corners where you have seen the cockroaches.

❊ Drive Ants Out of Your Home

To drive ants out of your house, you must mix crushed wild marjoram and wormwood together. Scatter this powder into all the corners of the house.

❊ Cleanse the House of Insects

To cleanse the house of insects, prepare a steeped infusion of walnut leaves. Wash the walls and floors with the infusion and repeat this charm as you do so:

> *Bedbugs, gather together and disappear from this home. Do not crawl along the walls, do not run across the floors, do not hide in the cracks. Be gone to dense forests, where people do not walk, beasts do not roam, birds do not fly. Those who remain will die a cruel death.*

❊ Expel Vermin from Home and Garden

To expel mice, locusts, beetles, worms, and caterpillars from your house, from your garden, and from your yard, sweep them with an old broom, repeating the following words:

> *I sweep filth away with this broom. I expel all creeping, crawling creatures. You will all cling to this broomstick. You will follow it, trail in its wake to where people do not walk and beasts do not roam, to where only creeping, crawling creatures live.*

After that, go to a deserted place, dragging the broom on the ground so that it leaves a trail behind it. Leave it there and, without looking back, return home.

SPELLS TO FIND A LOST ITEM

❋ Find a Lost Item in Your Home

If you have lost something in your home and cannot find it, put dried motherwort, lavender, and wormwood in a copper cup, sprinkle them with alcohol, and set them on fire. Use the herbal smoke to smudge all the rooms of the house. Very soon your lost item will reveal itself.

❋ Find a Lost Item Using a Candle

Put a purple candle in the center of the house on a perfectly flat surface and envision the lost object in your mind. Carefully follow the burning of the candle. The side of the candle where the melted wax is flowing down will show you in what direction you should begin searching.

❋ Find a Lost Item Using a Stone

To find a lost object, you must apply three drops of bergamot or eucalyptus oil on beryl stone or any other greenish stone. Clasp it between your palms and imagine the lost object, its shape and size. Then wait for spontaneous thoughts and visions that will show you where your lost item is.

SPELLS FOR WANTED AND UNWANTED GUESTS

❋ Spell for a Slowpoke

If you are waiting for a person to arrive but they are not turning up, stick a pin into the handle of a broom from above and place it at the front door. This simple sorcery will make a slowpoke hurry.

❋ Spell to Get Guests to Leave

If you invited friends or relatives to stay with you for a while but they have overstayed their welcome and are not planning to leave for some time, it may be uncomfortable for you to suggest that they leave. If you would still like for them to leave, you must do the following: Smudge all the rooms in your home with the smoke of smoldering chicory. In addition, sprinkle an infusion of thistle under their beds. For a stronger effect, spray their sheets with the infusion.

❊ Spell to Make an Unwanted Guest Forget the Way to Your Home

To make an unwanted guest forget the way to your home, after they leave sprinkle powder made from cloves, bay leaves, and garlic leaves over the threshold. If this does not help and the visitor returns, throw a pinch of the powder you made in both of the unwanted visitor's shoes.

❊ Spell to Prevent Unwanted Guests

To avoid having unwanted visitors, sprinkle a powder made from dried wild primrose over your threshold. Do not forget to sweep away the remainder of the powder after a few days, when you are ready to receive guests again.

❊ Spell to Avoid Running into People

If you wish to avoid unnecessarily running into people, dealing with relationships and unpleasant conversations, coat the handle of your front door with juice squeezed from the aromatic leaves of geraniums. You can do this with the leaves themselves by strongly pressing them against the handle.

PREVENTION AND PUNISHMENT OF THEFT

❊ Protect Your Home from Uninvited Guests and Thieves

To protect your home from uninvited guests and thieves, bury a knife deep in the ground with the point upward. Grease the hinges and door handles in your house with bergamot or hemp oil. Find as many old keys as there are doors in your house. Approach each door, touch it with a key, and repeat the following charm:

I lock the door with a key, I lock it with words, I lock it away from sly people, all the doors, all that is good, everything that is mine.

After that, tie all the keys together with a red ribbon and store them in a secret place.

❋ Spell to Prevent Theft

As you leave the house, hit the floor three times with the blunt end of a broom and say:

Everything is locked up, everything is shut. You cannot see inside, you cannot take anything from this place.

❋ Protect Your Property

If you go away, whether on vacation, for a visit, or on a business trip, and are concerned for your property, this prayer will help to protect your house. When you leave, before you lock the door, you must take the keys in your hands and whisper the following words:

I, [name], speak these words in blessing. This key [or keys] was forged to defend this house, to call angels and archangels that they may fly and with their holy power protect the key's strong seal. Dark forces will not break through, not with an ax, nor with a hammer, nor with spells. I lock the house with this key; I consecrate it with the sign of the cross, so that the evil eye cannot touch me, and the thief-robber will pass me by. So be it!

❋ Prevent Theft Using Salt

To prevent home theft, walk around the house, sprinkling the ground with salt and repeating the following charm:

I invoke the white salt, I call upon the black earth. I lock everything away, lock this house, this yard, this threshold. Neither a daytime trickster nor a thief who steals under cover of night will take anything from me. Everything I envision will come to pass, all my words will become deeds. Those deeds will not disappear into the ages; they will not be destroyed.

Afterward, go into your house, throw a pinch of salt in each room, and say:

> *The house is full of salt, the house is full of people, the house is full of things. Theft will not happen, nothing will be stolen, this charm will see to that.*

❊ Amulet to Protect the House

This amulet will protect your home from thieves. Dry and grind into powder garlic, finely chopped juniper branches, aspen bark, cumin seeds, and dried elderberries. Mix them all in equal parts. Pour the resulting mixture into a blue pouch. Then, insert three pins with black heads and three steel nails into the pouch. Hang this amulet over the front door and say the following charm:

> *In this house, there will be no theft, no robbery, no burglary. I trust in these herbs; I affirm the words of this charm; I cloak myself in secret. All those who are good may come in, but every sly person who dares to come must pass by. He will not enter my house, will not filch my belongings, will not stuff his pockets, nor will he fill his bags and pouches. So shall it always be.*

❊ Spell to Find the Identity of a Thief

To find the identity of a thief or determine where the missing item is, you need to put three sunflower seeds under your pillow. Then in a dream you will learn what you wish to know. Instead of sunflower seeds, you can also use three bay leaves.

❊ Spell to Make a Thief Return Stolen Goods

Because this ritual will punish the thief, be sure to consider before performing these actions whether the thing you have lost may have been accidentally taken by your relative or friend without any malicious intent.

To make the thief return the stolen goods, or at least ensure that he is sorely tormented by mental and physical pain, you must light a blue candle. Imagine that this is the thief, and if you know his name, write it on the candle. Prick the flame of the candle several times with a sharp needle. Next, you must burn something related to the stolen object over the candle's flame. For example, if your shoes were stolen, burn a shoe. If your purse was snatched, heat a coin over the fire.

❋ Spell to Punish a Thief

Put seven knives on the table, all pointing in different directions, and say:

> *As at sea, there is a wrought-iron trunk on a river that contains seven steel knives, seven brother-protectors. I open that trunk, I take out those knives, I direct them to their work. Go, knives, to [full name], to the one who committed the evil, who put their hands upon goodness. Cut him up and down, cut him across, so that his theft returns to him, so that nothing of his is hidden. My word is true, my work is fast, everything is said, everything is done.*

7 Health and Healing Spells

As long as humankind has existed on Earth, various ailments and sicknesses have plagued our species. Modern medicine, of course, has achieved unprecedented progress and can cure the vast majority of currently known diseases. But in the old days, our great-grandmothers turned to the help of common household medicine and often combined it with old world magic, using healing spells to treat diseases. Even now magic is used by some people as an unconventional method of getting rid of ailments. Magic is used to cure diseases and help exhausted patients every day; sometimes even life is saved. How do you save yourself or loved ones when doctors can't?

SPELLS TO CURE SICKNESS

Cure Diseases in Early Autumn

To cure any disease in early autumn, when the leaves have just begun to fall from the trees, you must approach one of the trees and say:

As all the leaves fall from this tree, so will this sickness disappear.
As time passes, what I say shall come to pass.

Every day, go to the tree you have chosen and repeat these words.

❋ Get Rid of Pain and Disease

To get rid of any pain and disease, smear your saliva or blood on a piece of bread and say the following words:

Lord of bread, take my sin, my sickness, my pain.

Then feed this bread to an animal.

❋ Remove Sickness Using Mustard Plant

Plant mustard seed in a pot and water it. Add the patient's blood or saliva. When the plant has grown, pull it out of the ground and apply it to the area of injury/sickness. Afterward, throw the plant into a swift-moving river or burn it over fire.

❋ Remove Sickness Using a Hard-Boiled Egg

Tell the patient to carry a hard-boiled egg for nine days. Then finely crush this egg and mix it with seventy-seven millet seeds. The patient should go to a river and throw the egg and seeds into it after uttering the following charm:

Sickness, I give these seventy-seven seeds to you. Eat your fill and leave me be!

❋ Spell to Cure Any Illness

To cure any illness, write its name on a piece of paper. Then cut off one letter each day and burn it, saying the following charm:

As this word dwindles, so does its meaning dwindle.

The name of the illness can also be written on a tear-off calendar. Write the name in full on the first page of the calendar, then write it without the last letter on the next page, then without the last two letters on the next, and so on. The sick person must be the one to tear off and burn the calendar sheets.

❋ Remove Illness Using Water and Wax

If you suffer from an illness, hold a glass filled with pure springwater over the area of the illness or injury. Drip melted red candle wax into the water and read the following charm:

> *Where there is bright fire, there is neither curse nor evil eye,*
> *neither starvation nor torment. Be gone, all sickness and infirmity,*
> *from blessed body, hot blood, racing heart, and flesh!*

Then anoint the area of injury with the water, saying:

> *Where there is holy water, there is neither curse nor evil eye,*
> *neither starvation nor torment.*

If the disease is internal, then you must drink three sips of this water.

❋ How to Determine If a Treatment Was Effective

Sew a small pouch from rare cloth. In the evening, before sunset, hard boil an egg. Without allowing the egg to cool, remove its shell and put the egg in the pouch. Tie the pouch with a red cord. Hang the pouch with the egg around your neck so that it lies directly under your tongue and go to bed.

In the morning remove the pouch from your neck and look at the egg. If it is white, it means that the treatment was successful and you do not need to repeat it. If the egg white is rotten or completely gone and the yolk has become completely black, then repeat the treatment until the egg is whole and white. Bury the used eggs and pouches in the ground.

❋ Spell to Destroy Diseases

Cut twelve twigs from a new broom with an ax. As you do so, say the following charm:

> *Twelve twigs I chop, twelve diseases I destroy.*

Afterward, you must put the chopped twigs in boiling water. When the water cools, pour it over the patient and say:

As water ebbs and flows away, so all sickness ebbs and flows away from [name].

❋ Spell to Beat a Disease

Remove excess hoof from the front leg of a horse, dry it, and grind it into powder. Add this powder to a sick person's drink and speak the following charm:

As a horse's hoof beats against earth and stone, so will this disease be beaten. As a horse runs swiftly, so will this disease quickly leave [name].

❋ Spell to Remove a Disease in Nine Days

Place valerian root into a pouch. Tell the patient to wear it for nine days and read the following charm:

In nine days, in nine nights, let this herb remove all aches and atrophy from [name]. Do not remain in white bone, red blood, head, stomach, back, chest, front, back, or in any living flesh. My words will not be forgotten, and in nine days all will be done.

When the time has passed, throw this pouch into a fire.

❋ Spell to Save and Protect the Patient

Light a white wax candle and pour springwater into a cup. Then take the candle in your right hand, the cup in your left, and walk around the ill person. Always keep the patient on your right side. As you do so, tilt the candle over the cup so that its melted wax drips into the water and read the following charm:

Lord of the earth, lord of the sea, lord of the heavens, save and protect [name]. With bright fire, with holy water, with enchanted words, as sure as sure can be, remove and destroy all fear and injury, all struggles and suffering. All of them, whether devised in the morning, spoken in the afternoon, or performed at night. This is my word and my bond, and neither the trickster nor the sage will change it.

Afterward, have the patient drink this water in small sips so as not to swallow the wax. After completing the treatment, bury the wax and cup in a deserted place.

❊ Talisman for When You Feel Unwell

If you feel unwell, take a large walnut, break it in half, and take out its core and all its septa. Put a spider in the shell and glue the halves of the nut together. Tie thread around the nut and wear it resting against your skin so that it is at your stomach. You should wear this talisman without removing it for one day and one night, and then bury it deep in the earth in a place where neither people nor beasts walk.

❊ Amulet to Prevent Contagious Diseases

To protect yourself from disease, cut a large stalk of straw into four pieces and then tie the four pieces of straw together with red thread. Put three small wheat grains into one of the pieces, a little salt in another, and ground incense into the third. Seal the ends of these three pieces with wax so that their contents do not fall out and scatter. Pass the red thread through the fourth piece. Wear this amulet around your neck to protect against all contagious diseases.

❊ Spell to Steal Health and Beauty to Your Advantage

During the waning moon, buy a small mirror, immediately wrap it with a black handkerchief and do not look at it until the beginning of the ritual. First prepare thirteen completely black wax candles (it is preferable for you to make your own).

At night on an altar or a table covered with a black tablecloth, place the candles in a circle. Unwrap the mirror and put it in the center, with the reflective surface facing up. Light the candles counterclockwise, starting from where you stand. Above each say aloud:

A devil's wheel and hellfire!
Demons and devils, hanged and drowned men,
Come to me, join me for a daring deal!

When all the candles are lit, take the mirror in your left hand, look directly into the eyes of your reflection, and read:

> *I conjure with hellfire, I close with a devil's wheel*
> *Demons and devils, hanged and drowned men!*
> *At this hour you will appear, you will settle in the mirror.*
> *My illness and sickness, sadness and sorrow,*
> *Take it from me, bury it in the mirror.*
> *Keep it until someone looks in the mirror, then give it to them.*
> *Bring health and beauty to me!*
> *Hellfire and a devil's wheel*
> *Locked and sealed, I conjure you.*
> *This very hour do as I command!*

Immediately wrap the mirror in the handkerchief and put it back in the center of the circle. Leave the candles to burn out. The next night, bury the candles in an unmarked grave and throw the mirror at the victim. Whoever you choose must look at the mirror.

SPELLS TO GET RID OF WARTS

❊ Get Rid of Warts Using Thread and Potato

Tie knots in a yellow silk thread. Hold it over each wart and say the following charm each time:

> *As this thread does not untie, so you, blight, will not grow on [name].*

Then slice into a small potato and put the knotted thread into the cut. Bury the potato in the ground so that no one knows about it. When it rots, all the warts will disappear.

❊ Get Rid of Warts Using Toad and Thread

Find a forest toad, count all its warts and tie as many knots in a woolen thread as there are warts on both you and the toad. Release the toad into the forest and discard the knotted thread at the crossroad of two footpaths. The first person to step over this thread will take all your warts on himself.

❋ Get Rid of Warts Using a Wheat Stalk

Cut the grains from a wheat stalk. Prick a wart with the sharp end of the stem and say the following charm:

As this straw withers and decays, so this wart will wither away.

Plant the stalk in the damp ground with the stem facing up. When the stalk sprouts, the wart will disappear.

❋ Get Rid of Warts Using an Apple

Cut an apple in half with a strong thread. Rub the warts with both halves of the apple, saying the following charm:

As this apple is not in one piece, so we will not be of a piece with you.

Put the apple halves together and tie them with a thread. Dip the apple into manure or dirt and continue the charm:

As this apple decays, so will the wart be gone.

As soon as the apple rots, the warts will disappear.

❋ Get Rid of Warts Using Fatback

Cook a piece of cured fatback (called САЛО in Russian) in pea broth. Anoint the wart with the fatback, then give the fatback to a stray dog.

❋ Heal a Wart Using Dandelion Juice

To heal a wart quickly, you must rub it every day with dandelion juice; you can substitute celandine juice, crabapple or rowan berries, sliced garlic, or onions.

❋ Get Rid of Warts Using Gray Thread

Wrap the finger with the wart on it with gray thread and say:

As I twist and turn the strong gray thread, you will neither rise nor grow!

Remove the thread from your finger and throw it into the toilet.

SPELLS FOR GETTING RID OF BAD HABITS

❊ Get Rid of Bad Habits in Nine Days

To get rid of bad habits in nine days, mix fennel seeds into olive oil and use it to coat a black candle. Hold the candle and envision all the power of your destructive desire flowing into it. Then, put the candle on a table and light its wick. As it burns, you must imagine that as the candle melts away, so does your dependence on the habits you wish to end. Envision the fire burning away all your bad attachments and cleansing your inner self. After the candle burns out completely and extinguishes, discard all the remaining wax or paraffin in a deserted place, as far as possible from your house.

❊ Get Rid of Bad Habits Using Fire

Describe all that you want to get rid of on a piece of paper. Pour alcohol into a shallow bowl and set it on fire. Roll the paper into a ball and throw it into the fire. Envision that the fiery flame destroys the strength of your addictions and that they now have no power over you.

❊ Get Rid of Complications

To get rid of whatever complicates your life, use a symbol of your problem. For example, take a cigarette butt, a wine-bottle stopper, excess food, or a piece of paper with a description of what you want to get rid of, and throw it in a fire. As it burns, speak the following charm:

> *With this bright fire, with this sacred flame I rid myself of*
> *[smoking, drunkenness, etc.] forever and forever.*

Imagine the fire destroying the power that enslaved you. Know that it now has no power over you and that you will become free and happy.

❊ Get Rid of Vices Using Sour Apple

Pick a sour, unripe apple from its tree. Bite into it three times. Each bite represents the power of your bad habits passing into to the apple. Then, bury the apple in the ground, imagining that you are burying all your worst vices.

❋ Get Rid of Habits Using Salt

Go out to a field in windy weather. Grab a handful of salt and imagine that the power associated with your habit is absorbed into this salt through your palms. Begin to unclench your hands slowly so that the salt spills out onto the ground in a small stream and is carried away by the wind. Wipe your palms against each other so that not a single grain of salt remains. Then you can be sure that you have completely gotten rid of the shackles of your previous vices.

❋ Get Rid of Addictions

To get rid of addictions, as well as unwanted feelings and excessive emotions, go to a deserted place and light a blue candle. Then, sprinkle salt on the ground to create a circle around yourself. You must draw this circle clockwise. Put a candle in the center of the circle, then step out of it. Imagine that you are leaving not only the candle but also all of your negative desires behind you in the circle. After that, making sure the candle burns out completely, go home and do not say hello to anyone or talk until you cross the threshold of your home.

8 Dreams and Divinations

Our ancestors believed that when we dream at night our souls leave our bodies and travel the world. Those nights when the soul did not travel far from its body were considered empty. The moon cycle also affects our dreams.

We can see most prophetic dreams on a growing (waxing) moon, and they show us our future. Empty nights are more likely to tell us about the past than about the future, carrying the information absorbed during our lives. People see such dreams on the waning moon, which symbolizes the past. And, of course, any prophecy will come true in the full moon, when the moon has gained its strength and entered into close contact with the Earth.

People who have strong intuition dream more often, and it is not necessary to perform magic to have a prophetic dream. Many do not remember their dreams, or remember them only for a split second in the middle of the night and in the morning they are often forgotten. Using a spell or ritual for prophetic dreaming is a great opportunity to know your future. Prophetic dreams can give a person the information that one needs to make the right decision or protect oneself.

SPELLS FOR PROPHETIC DREAMS

❊ Prophetic Dreams

To have a prophetic dream, tie a simple knot in a heavy thread, but do not tighten it. Put this thread under your pillow. If the dream predicts happiness, then, when you wake up in the morning, tighten the knot. If the dream predicts unhappiness, undo the knot.

❊ Prophetic Dreams Using a Mirror

Before you go to bed, put a laurel leaf under each leg of the bed, conceal a small round mirror under your pillow, and say:

> *As darkness and light are reflected in this mirror, so will my future be reflected in it.*

You will dream of a mirror, which will reflect the upcoming events. When you wake up in the morning, hide the mirror in a secluded place and store it there in secret and security. Remember that if the mirror breaks, this will not affect your life in the best possible way, so place it carefully.

❊ Tea for Prophetic Dreams

Use this recipe to make tea for prophetic dreams. Mix together equal parts dried lemon balm, plantain seeds, and willow bark. Pour one spoonful of this mixture into a glass of hot water. When the infusion cools, strain it and drink exactly half. Set the remaining half of the brew underneath the head of your bed, and then immediately go to sleep.

❊ How to Make Your Dreams Come True

Fill a small pouch made of light blue fabric with the following items and dried herbs: holly, heliotrope, jasmine, mimosa, nails, sage, lavender, and pine needles. You are not required to use all of the items listed—use what you can find. Write the description of an event that you want to see in a dream on a sheet of paper, and put the paper into the pouch. Put the pouch under your pillow and go to bed.

What you see in your sleep will tell you what to do and how to proceed to make your dreams come true.

❋ Spell to Obtain a Definite Answer

Write a question that you have long wanted a definite answer to on a pink sheet of paper. Toss three pinches of dried fern onto the paper and roll it into a tube. Wrap the tube with white thread but do not tie any knots in it. Put the note under your pillow, and then you will learn the answer to your question in your dream.

DIVINATIONS

❋ Divination Using Hazelnuts

Draw a circle a foot in diameter on the ground. Pick up thirteen hazelnuts. Shake them in your fists and mentally ask the question that interests you. Then throw the nuts up over the circle you drew. If most of the nuts fall into the circle, this means that the answer to your question is positive, and if they fall outside it, it means that most likely what you want will not come to pass. Then, try to interpret what shape the nuts are making, and what it might mean. You may see the first letters of a word important to the fulfillment of your dream or the outline of an omen that indicates how you need to act to make your wish come true.

❋ Divination Using a Burning Stick

Determine your future in the burning of a stick. Set fire to a damp stick (you can dampen it or find a stick that is damp from the rain), saying the following charm:

> *The answer is in the flames, the truth is in the cinders.*

If a damp stick burns brightly, it foretells a long life; if it sparks, then a disease may be in your future; and if it suddenly goes out when you light it, expect great difficulties.

❋ Divination Using Bones

Put a large shoulder bone in the fire. After a while, take it out of the fire and look at the shapes and marks that appeared on it. The meaning of various figures can be determined in advance, or you can trust your intuition as you examine them. The first associations that arise in you at the sight of the sorcery tool will yield the most accurate prediction.

❋ Divination Using Wax

Before you go to bed any night of the week, put a small piece of wax (about half the size of your fist) into an unwashed sock. Conceal the sock at the head of your bed. Keep it there until Sunday morning, then remove the wax from the sock and melt the wax in a pot on the stove. Pour all the melted wax into a bowl filled with clean, cold water while asking aloud the question you want answered. Analyze the shape of the wax in the water. The first associations and interpretations that come to your head will indicate the answer to your question. If the future you predict suits you, wrap the wax in a white cloth and keep it as a mascot. If the wax form seems to predict an unfavorable future, bury the wax in the ground in a deserted place or throw it into a river.

❋ Divination Using a Book

Put an old book in front of you on a table. Think about the question for which you want the answer. Hold a needle in your right hand. Say your question aloud. Close your eyes, open the book on an arbitrary page, and pierce it with a needle. Open your eyes. The needle will indicate a word or phrase that will help determine the answer to your question.

❋ Fortune-Telling Using Oak Bark

You will need a piece of oak bark, which you must gather in autumn. Light a purple candle, put the tip of the bark into its flame, and say three times:

> *The answer is in the fire, the truth is in the bark.*

Throw the smoldering bark on a white plate and observe it as it crumbles, repeating the charm until the bark stops smoking. Look closely at the burned edges of the bark. Try to discern various shapes and bumps. Maybe you will see a galloping horse, the outline of buildings, or a child playing in a yard. Try to understand the meaning of these figures and what they mean for you personally.

❋ Divination Using a Hazel Branch

At sunrise, cut off a forklike branch without fruit from a wild hazel tree. As you do so, say the following charm:

> *I cut off this branch to determine the future, the present, and the past; to find buried treasures, underground waters, and missing things. The whole truth is in the trunk, the whole truth is in my hand, everything lies in the distance. As I say it, it shall come to pass and never be forgotten.*

To predict or search for different omens, you must hold this nut branch with a forked end in each hand and, keeping it parallel to the ground, walk around and ask questions. If the branch stays still, the answer is negative. If the free end moves up or down it indicates a positive response to your questions and expectations.

9

Cemetery Traditions, Superstitions, Sorcery, and Spells

The majority of people have never particularly loved cemeteries or burials. There are unpleasant events associated with the loss of those close to us, as well as a lot of superstitions and legends. In the end, the cemetery reminds many of us of our own mortality. This attitude toward burials has a basis in reason. The gathering of a large number of dead in a relatively small area; reburial over existing graves; the suffering, fear, and pain that people experience when they visit the cemetery—all of this has led to the formation of a special cemetery atmosphere. Of course, this atmosphere affects everything that enters it, whether it is people, dead bodies, or omens, not to mention the things that are found directly next to the graves.

The grave is the resting place of the body of the deceased. The grave is considered a shrine that cannot be defiled. You cannot curse it, plow it, or, even worse, dig it up to steal whatever items remain. It is forbidden not only to take things left in a grave but also to throw something at it (for example, dirt when you are in the process of digging another grave).

Sorceresses all over the world have long appreciated the magical properties of cemetery land. We will explore this topic later in this chapter. But first we'll discuss the Slavic beliefs and customs surrounding death and the afterlife.

AFTERLIFE BELIEFS

Slavic people believe that when a person's heart stops, the separation of the astral body from the physical body takes place. This can also occur during operations under general anesthesia and in 75 percent of cases during labor. In the case of a lethal outcome, the link between the physical and astral planes is broken forever.

The astral body is called the soul, which continues to be near the human physical body for up to forty days. During this time, the astral body has its information copied as it prepares for the next incarnation. If the person, or the relatives, prepared in advance for the death and funeral, then a strong energy-information channel is automatically bestowed upon the next incarnation. Errors that are not corrected and not worked out in this life are copied in the following incarnation cycles (lives). This is what is called karma.

Pagan Slavs believe that there are three changes the body of the deceased undergoes at three specific times:

day three, its appearance changes
day nine, it begins to decay
day forty, its heart rots

These physical changes are mirrored by three tests in the spiritual realm. On the way to the kingdom of God, the soul undergoes the test of spirits according to its earthly deeds. These tests are called "trials" and usually begin on the third day after death. All that exists (according to Christian mythology) is a series of judgments. The soul is denounced by demons for its sins as it travels. Each trial (ordeal) corresponds to a certain sin. Evil spirits are called tax collectors. In total, there are twenty ordeals corresponding to each group of sins depending on how grave they are (for example, a sin of words, lies, condemnation and slander, gluttony, laziness, stealing, avarice, stinginess, covetousness, untruth, envy, pride and vanity, rage and anger, murder, sorcery, fornication, adultery, depravity, etc.), based upon the main human vices.

Saint Macarius of Alexandria says, as the Angel revealed to him, that after worshipping God on the third day the soul is allowed to see the various abodes of the saints and the beauty of paradise. The soul watches all these things for six days, admiring the beauty and forgetting the grief it felt when it was bound to its body.

On the ninth day, relatives pray for the deceased so that his soul will be bestowed with the honor given the sainthood and receive the reward of heavenly bliss.

If it is guilty of sin, the soul begins to mourn and reproach itself for spending its life carelessly and not serving God as it should. After it has observed paradise, the soul (on the ninth day of its separation from the body) ascends to worshipping God.

The number forty is a landmark often found in the Holy Scriptures. According to the same Saint Macarius, after that second worship, the Lord commands that the soul be shown hell with all its torments. For thirty days the soul, driven by the torments of hell, trembles for fear that it would have such a fate.

On the fortieth day the trials end, and the soul rises for the third time to worship God. God then passes judgment and determines where the soul will be placed in anticipation of the Last Judgment. This judgment is formed according to its earthly deeds, as well the prayers of the church and the deceased's loved ones during these forty days.

The judgment on the fortieth day is an individual judgment to determine the position of the soul. According to the teachings of the Orthodox Church, a soul's position can change according to the prayers, alms, and good deeds of relatives and friends given in memory of the deceased.

BURIAL TRADITIONS OF EASTERN SLAVS

The grave of the deceased is dug in a place chosen in advance by relatives or by the deceased in life. People close to the deceased are usually forbidden to dig a grave, including the wife of the deceased as well as any women who have recently lost one of their relatives. Instead, the digging is done for free by the old or beggars, who avoid talking about the deceased. If preexisting graves are found when they are digging the new grave, the gravediggers throw money and other valuable things there so that the dead people will not be upset and "drive away" the newcomer.

Meanwhile, the women ritually wash the corpse with water. When the gravediggers finish the work, they call for the women to be brought out so that the women can pour the water used to wash the corpse into the grave.

The coffin is brought out of the house, and grain is poured over it. Then the coffin is brought to the grave site. If the grave turns out to be too small for the coffin and has to be expanded, it means that soon afterward a new dead person will enter the burial place, usually a relative of the deceased. This explanation was also given when the grave was too large: they believe that one victim was not enough and the next one will soon appear. An especially dangerous incident is if a grave collapses and one of the dead falls.

The grain that was poured on the coffin when it was carried out of the house is swept away. The boarded-up coffin is lowered into the grave on ropes or on long, wide towels so that the road to "the light" is wide, like a canvas. In the Russian North, the coffin is placed vertically in the grave with hemp rope. As the coffin is lowered, those present throw various things at the grave: money (for the deceased to buy a place in the cemetery in the otherworld), clothes (kerchiefs, scarves, belts), canvas used for sewing a shroud, as well as needles and threads (for sorcery). In the grave, as well as in the coffin, they place objects that the one who died loved in life (for example, tools for artisans, etc.). Southern Russians sprinkle wine and oil over the grave. Many Slavs retain the custom of smashing pottery and placing it in the grave. They might, for example, smash the vessel in which they brought wine and oil.

In many areas of Ukraine and Belarus, the custom of "stamping a grave" continues: a Ukrainian priest sings while using a special iron spade to mark a cross over the grave and across the ground. Belarusians do the same by dropping the coffin into a pit or a piled-up hill that has already been stamped from four corners crosswise with a shovel. The burial is considered incomplete without such stamping: failing to do so would allow the deceased to leave the grave and wander as a ghost.

After burial, they immediately make a cross over the grave. At least a small, temporary cross is placed, until they make a new one that is the same size as a person.

On the grave of a child that is born dead, a fire is lit from aspen branches. On the grave of an unbaptized child, a stone or a triangle made from an aspen tree is left. At the grave of a suicide, a stone is left; their graves are arranged outside the cemetery. Russians place suicides in remote places and ravines, and Belarusians place them at crossroads and hillocks in the forest so that they can be seen from everywhere. In Transcarpathia, suicides are usually buried at the scene of their death, and people throw stones at the gravesites.

A grave is often made in the form of a house as a sign that it is the eternal home of the deceased. The Russians install crosses on the graves with a gable cover and with the icon sometimes bearing the name "chapel." In the Russian North, in addition to the usual cross, one can see an oblong quadrangular structure on the top or a flat roof on which

Fig. 9.1. A grave marked by an orthodox cross with a roof, which symbolizes "home"

Fig. 9.2. A cemetery in a rural village in Russia

a cross is placed. On the grave they also create a kind of garden: they plant flowers and fruit trees.

MEMORIAL CUSTOMS

Memorial feasts took place in ancient times, when pagans broke bread at the graves of their dead tribesmen. Military games, competitions, dances, songs, lamentations, and feasts were all included. It was also meant as a kind of ritual help for the sake of the deceased, for support and to ask God to receive the soul. The memorial was conducted directly next to the burial site or funeral pyre of the deceased before and after the main rite. The memorial has three parts, which coincide with the path of the soul to the next world. This tradition found its way into Christian rituals—memorials are interpreted in Holy Scriptures as a type of Christian alms for those who gather—and ancient Christian memorial feasts later transformed into the modern-day wake. They would memorialize the deceased on other days of the year as well (after half a year, a year, and on the deceased's birthday or saint's day). There are also wake ceremonies known as calendar memorials, which are associated with certain holidays. These ceremonies follow the economic and household customs of peasants and are included in church rituals. The church could not overcome the pagan-Slavic beliefs and customs, so it adapted and included pagan holidays and traditions.

The memorial service for the ninth day, fortieth day, and one year following a death usually consists of relatives of the deceased visiting the cemetery and a memorial feast for the guests held in the home of the deceased.

According to the rules of the church, the symbolic meaning of a memorial on the third day after death is that the deceased was baptized in the name of the Father, the Son, and the Holy Spirit and believed in the Triune God, the Trinity Uniform and Indivisible. The living then beseech the Holy Trinity to forgive the deceased for any sins committed by word, deed, and thought and take into account the three virtues: faith, hope, and love.

This symbolism holds great meaning for Orthodox believers in the face of the unknown, the soul's afterlife. When Saint Macarius of Alexandria, as it is written in the Holy Scriptures, asked the Angel accompanying him through the desert to explain the significance of the church memorial on the third day, the Angel replied that during the first two days the soul, with the angels present, is allowed to walk on Earth where it chooses. A well-loved soul wanders around the house where its body rests like a bird looking for its nest. A virtuous soul walks where it has done good works. On the third day, in imitation of Christ, the soul ascends to heaven to worship God.

The fortieth day was the most important occasion. It was believed that after forty days the soul goes far away, and so those attending hurried to do everything by that time. They requested a memorial liturgy (a requiem or a forty-hour devotion in the church), and they gave something in the soul's memory and in the church's name. On the fortieth day, they always gave money for the service.

After the burial of a dead family member, close relatives would attend a memorial gathering along with acquaintances, coworkers, and friends of the deceased. Those who are not invited should not try to attend, because it can be assumed that the family may be experiencing some financial difficulties due to the sudden expenses. The family may also decide that they only want a small circle of people to attend. Those who attend bring food, consisting of rice pudding, or *kanun,* as well as pancakes, pies, honey drink, and so on, and leave it at the grave. The remains of dishes are often left on the grave and given to the poor.

In some regions, inviting others to the memorials was not done. Anyone who was a close acquaintance or coworker of the deceased in life could come to the gathering. To attend demonstrated respect for the deceased and the family. They would formally invite the clergy—in reality, however, they would try to discourage them from taking part. At one time, however, the wretched and poor were required to attend as well. Those who washed and dressed the deceased were expressly invited.

When they arrived home from a burial, they had to wash their hands and dry them with a towel. People also ritually cleansed themselves by touching their hands to the stove or to bread. Before that, they would even specially warm up the bath, bathe in it, and put on new clothes.

Up until the time the deceased was taken to the cemetery and interred, a meal would be prepared in the home. People would also try to clean the house before the deceased was taken to the grave, but it was difficult to be sure how much time there would be. They rearranged furniture and washed the floors. They swept any dust or trash that accumulated over three days from the corners of the house to the threshold, then burned it. They had to wash the floors thoroughly in the corners and at the threshold. They cleaned every doorknob as well. After they cleaned a room they would smudge it with frankincense or juniper.

The memorial feast in Orthodox tradition is considered part of the service, so even eating the food follows the rules and tradition for a memorial. Observing the norms in Orthodox memorial feasts requires that, before it begins, one of the people close to the deceased reads the seventeenth Kathisma from the Psalter and then lights a lamp or candle. Immediately before eating, they read "Our Father . . ."

There is a tradition to set the deceased's place at the feast table (they may place a knife and fork parallel to each other on an empty plate), light a candle (often decorated with a black ribbon at the base), and place a glass of vodka covered with a piece of black bread.

The tradition to set a place with food at the table, along with the tradition to cover mirrors, windows, and television screens, have nothing to do with Orthodoxy. This tradition has its roots in paganism, but it is widely used in modern life. This example and many others prove that the modern burial and memorial ritual is syncretistic, as it involves many components of Slavic folk culture, which is an integral part of Orthodoxy.

Folk tradition regulated the order in which people sat at the memorial table. The host and head of the family usually sat at the head of the table. Relatives sat on both sides of the table in order of closeness in kinship and seniority. As a rule, children had their place at the end of the table. In certain situations, the deceased's relatives may wish for children to sit close to their father or mother (on either side), such as when one of their parents has died. The place where the deceased person usually sat was left unoccupied, its back decorated with a mourning ribbon or a spruce branch.

After the guests departed, the members of the household usually bathed before sunset if time allowed. They did not have to clear the table. Instead, they tried to cover the cutlery and the rest of the food with something. The only place that they did not cover was intended for the deceased. At night, they firmly closed all the doors and windows. At dusk they tried not to cry so that they would not "call the deceased from the cemetery," according to popular belief.

The ancient Slavs believed that the richer and more splendid the farewell to the deceased was, the better he would live in the otherworld. Vanity, prestige, and the financial status of the deceased's family all figured into the display. Another factor in the amount of money involved in a memorial was ignorance of the church's ruling in such matters.

Currently, these memorials are still similar to the pagan feasts that ancient Slavs held in honor of the deceased. In real life, these memorials rarely take place without alcoholic beverages. These will usually be strong drinks (vodka, cognac, dry red wine). Sweet and sparkling alcoholic beverages are usually excluded. Alcoholic beverages are part of the feast in part because they help to relieve the emotional stress that comes with the loss of a relative or loved one. However, their presence is also reminiscent of pagan memorial feasts.

KUTYA: A TRADITIONAL FOOD OF THE DEAD

The tradition of making kutya originates long before the appearance of Christianity among the Slavic peoples. Kutya, according to most researchers, is an ancient pagan dish and is associated with rituals such as burial and sacrifice. Since it was believed that the deceased retained ordinary human needs, including the need for food, the ancient Slavs cooked wheat porridge for the deceased and left it on the grave.

The first mention of it was found in the manuscripts of the Byzantine Empire and dates back to the fifth or sixth centuries CE. Like any other traditional dish, kutya has a certain value in itself—first of all due to the ingredients included in it. Grain—steamed or boiled—meant the resurrection of the dead. After it falls into the ground and germinates, a new life emerges from it. The very same grain decays. Something like this happens with the body of the deceased.

Honey and raisins from our ancestors were considered not only symbols of health and wealth, they also symbolized the pleasure of the bliss of eternal life in the kingdom of heaven. Thus, the three simple ingredients of kutya signified immortality, resurrection, and the bliss of eternal life.

I also mentioned health and prosperity. Why is that? The fact is that both the kutya for the memorial and the Christmas kutya were being prepared. The latter was served on the table three times—on Kolyady, Christmas, and baptism. Accordingly, poor (lean) kutya was prepared, then rich (generous) kutya, followed by hungry (watery) kutya. It was believed that the thicker the porridge turned out, the richer and more agreeably the family would live the next year.

Kutya is prepared and served for a commemoration. It is always the first dish on the table and should be consecrated in the church after the funeral service of a deceased or at the memorial service. You can also sprinkle kutya with holy water before putting it on the memorial table.

After kutya, guests were offered Lenten memorial pancakes and honey kissel. According to custom, kutya was always served with specially baked bread, which was broken by hands. It was absolutely forbidden to cut such bread with a knife.

Interestingly, such a custom existed in Belarus and is still practiced: having celebrated the Day of Remembrance, it is customary to hang a clean, new towel out of the window and put a plate with kutya and pancakes on it. It is believed that this will please the spirits of our departed ancestors.

MOURNING CUSTOMS

After the funeral of a loved one, many people, especially close relatives, would observe a period of mourning.

The deepest mourning was to be followed by a widow and lasted up to a year. In earlier times, they were only allowed to wear mostly black clothes without jewelry. Naturally, it would be considered indecent if the widow even entertained the thought of remarriage before the period of mourning ended.

A widower wore mourning for six months in most cases. Children had to mourn their dead parents for a year and gradually move from black to lighter shades of clothing. Mourning for a deceased father or mother was divided into deep mourning, which lasted six months, ordinary mourning, which lasted three months, and half mourning, which lasted the remaining three months. It was in these last three months that black clothes were mixed with white and gray. For deceased grandparents, it was customary to wear mourning for half a year. This period was also evenly split into deep and half mourning. The same term of mourning was observed for a deceased sister or brother.

Mourning clothes were dark, black or blue. Shades of red were completely excluded. More often than not, the clothes were new. Women should wear a headscarf during a period of mourning. In the modern day, people buy a black dress (or suit) and a headscarf if they do not have suitable clothes or headgear in their wardrobe. In earlier times, people did not even try to take special care of clothes used for mourning. According to popular belief, to take good care of that clothing was a sign of disrespect for the memory of the deceased.

There was a widespread custom during this period for women to not cut their hair, wear elegant curly hairstyles, or even, in some cases, braid their hair. Women were generally expected to show external signs of mourning for a longer period of time. Men could choose to wear black or dark-colored clothes only on memorial days and not be publically condemned for it, even in villages.

Signs of mourning would remain in the house for a long time depending on the mourner's way of life. In most cases, people would continue to observe mourning up to forty days, or even up to a year.

In the families of believers, those who mourned would do so by praying more intensely, reading religious books, fasting, and amusing themselves at home. They could not participate in various entertainments, such as holidays or gambling. If a relative's wedding occurred during a period of mourning, they would take off their mourning attire for the day of the ceremony. The next day, they would put it on again.

During deep mourning, it was not considered acceptable for people to go out in public to places of entertainment. Even going to the theater was considered permissible only after the complete removal of mourning clothes. If a person chose to end their mourning arbitrarily, it was considered a failure to observe folk traditions. Such a failure is immediately noted and could lead to the mourner being publically condemned.

In modern times, people do not usually mourn for as long as they once did, especially in the city. This varies from person to person and depends on a number of factors.

When people wear mourning, they should not display boundless grief to demonstrate it to others. They should conduct themselves with dignity, as the purpose of mourning is not only to show external piety or demonstrate one's mental state but also to show that the time is being spent in deep reflection about who one is as a person and the meaning of life. In the end, how we honor the memory of our relatives and others will also serve to honor our memories when we pass, for no one is meant to be forever in this world.

CONVENTIONS TO BE OBSERVED AT AND AFTER THE FUNERAL

The water that washed the body of the deceased is very often used to bring involuntary death, damage, or the destruction of the family or others. You cannot allow the body of a deceased, unknown person to be washed, since this water can then be used to cast a deadly curse by adding it to the food of a future victim. If this washing is done, it is better to take the water outside the house, into the yard, and pour it into a hole that you marked with a cross. It cannot even be poured out into a toilet bowl, as that can lead to the spread of disease.

Things that the deceased leaves behind bear a powerful negative energy from their former master. And no, dry cleaning will not remove it.

You cannot place the coffin in front of a threshold for public viewing, as it is possible that it will block the departure of the deceased and force them into the interfenestral space. You cannot look out the window at the deceased.

Do not allow flowers to be placed on the coffin that contains the body of the deceased. The flowers are to be thrown on the road the funeral procession travels. Taking these flowers could lead to the transfer of diseases from the dead to the living. You cannot collect these flowers, step on them, or bring them into the house.

Do not put icons in the coffin. There are crosses that are specially made to be placed in the hands of the deceased to serve this purpose.

You must wash your hands for the first time in the cemetery after you have grieved. As you do so, sprinkle the earth in the grave with the water three times and say, "You must rest in peace." You cannot pour dirt on a person's head, as it may lead to harm. You cannot pour dirt into someone's collar, even to ward off fear. You cannot throw the handkerchief you used to wipe your tears into the grave, or you will bring harm to yourself.

It is unacceptable to kiss a dead person on the forehead or lips. You may only kiss him on the "third eye," the space between the eyes, above the nose. Diseases can be transmitted to people who have similar energy. The younger the human body, the more accessible it is for the deceased's migrating essence, the so-called curse. Therefore, funerals should not be attended by children under three years old or pregnant women. And those who enjoy walking around cemeteries should remember that the grave and even an urn from the crematorium are powerful descending energy funnels. You should visit the cemetery as rarely as possible, and when you come home, wash your shoes thoroughly, wash your clothes, and wash yourself.

Used bindings (in Russia and Ukraine they used to bind the ankles and wrists of the dead person) from the hands and feet of the deceased are extremely widespread in sorcery. People are often advised to apply them to sore spots, or to sew them into their spouse or lover's clothes. It was believed to be a cure for very bad diseases. At the magical level, these bindings link the astral plane of the deceased person to the living person who has them. The deceased cannot go on to the next life and draws the living person after him. Over time though, those bindings lead to diseases, frequent quarrels, and scandals in families (this includes alcohol dependence in men, as well as nervous and mental disorders in family members). Therefore, it is very important that the bindings remain in the coffin. After they are removed, they are usually placed under the feet of the deceased. Handkerchiefs that are tied to the funeral procession perform the same function. They cannot be brought home.

According to the old canons (laws), the requiem or last rite (in Russian, отпевание) is given by the priest while the deceased is still in the house. The Russian term literally translates to "sing out," because more than half of the prayers are sung in it. It was established by the church to say farewell and wish good passage to another world. People take dirt from the cemetery to use in deadly spells (curses) by pouring it on a threshold, into pockets, or behind the collar of a victim. Everyone knows that the dirt taken from the cemetery after the funeral should not be brought into the home or left on a doorstep, otherwise the person is considered sealed, or buried—and the doorstep too. This will lead to people becoming ill.

Remember that nothing can be taken from the cemetery! This includes scarves and towels removed from the cross, or wreaths. A beautiful bouquet of real flowers or artificial flowers in a vase left on the grave can immediately be taken by the grandmother, who will sell them again, but with the appropriate conjuring charms. With the use of such flowers and vases, people can be spelled in a matter of hours. The victim may experience a sudden rise in temperature, weakness, vomiting, cramps, and fear. They may even die within a short period.

During the memorial week, you cannot take sweets, cookies, or eggs from the graves on a napkin, paper, or cellophane wrapper. Foods that lie on bare dirt or on a gravestone are meant for the deceased and cannot be eaten.

If a house contains a corpse, then very often people use glasses filled with water and wheat or salt instead of candlesticks to hold candles. If you sprinkle this wheat or salt on someone, you can put a curse on them. Also, you should not put any items on the deceased that belong to a member of the deceased's family. In addition, you cannot tie a knot before the deceased is removed from the house.

There is a tradition during the funeral procession to stop at crossroads and perform a brief Lity (the Orthodox memorial service) on the deceased. The dead person cannot cross the road otherwise. It will lead to the appearance of various growths and tumors in the people in the procession.

At the grave, the lid of the coffin is closed and sealed. The deceased is lowered with his feet to the east and his head to the west. Then the priest sprinkles the earth crosswise while reading the prayer. The ash from the censer is emptied into the grave, as well as the burnt oil from the lantern and candlesticks left by the deceased. Afterward the priest performs Lity, and the grave is covered with earth.

We bring breakfast to the cemetery every Sunday. After forty days, you must pour water under the cross in the morning when you bring breakfast to the cemetery. Then, crumble bread on the grave.

In general, curses can be cast on vodka at funerals, wakes, weddings, parties, and feasts. For example, at a funeral and a memorial service, there is always a pile of offerings for the deceased, covered with bread and salt. Vodka, which is usually in the pile, is intended for the deceased, but someone who wants to perform a curse can take it and us it for their sorcery. If someone drinks this vodka from the pile, you can be sure that the person will be afflicted by a strong curse toward alcohol dependence. You will hear him say, "I do not want to drink, but something makes me do it."

According to Christian tradition, when a person dies, the body must be buried; that is, sealed. When you stamp/seal the deceased, you must take the dirt to church for a special rite and then go to the cemetery only on a bright day and spread it in a cross shape over the grave. You cannot bring the dirt into the house or you will risk losing a loved one again.

HOW TO AVOID A CURSE AT A FUNERAL

A deceased person cannot be left alone in the house; women must be near the body. You must cover all mirrors in the house for forty days, and in the place where the deceased is, lay an ax so that no more deaths take place in the house. You cannot be late in handing out things forty days after the death. If the deceased left behind a widow or widower, you must take the engagement ring from the body to keep the one left behind from becoming sick. After the deceased is taken outside of the home, those still in the home must not bake bread, clean, or sweep the floor for forty days, because the soul is still present. After forty days you can clean the home as usual and remove sheets from the mirrors.

After the removal of the deceased from the house, it was often customary to turn over the table on which the coffin stood. It was believed that this prevents the deceased from returning. Pregnant women do not wash the deceased and do not follow the coffin if it is possible for such a woman to stay at home.

Do not offer the deceased photos of yourself or those close to you (otherwise it will cause illness); do not offer your belongings, your crosses. Try to prevent anyone from putting such things in the coffin without your knowledge. Do not give anyone a rope or binding that was associated with the legs and hands of the deceased, or use the water that was used to wash the deceased, as this water can be very damaging.

In villages, the bed where the person died was not burned but taken to the hen coop for three days so that "the rooster would sing over it thrice." There are sorceresses who suggest that others lie down on the bed of the deceased to relieve pain in the spine. Do not do this, as it can cause harm. Sometimes sorceresses will follow a coffin backward. You must be careful to follow them to make sure that they do not do so. And some will tie knots while the corpse is being removed. Whatever they say, they are causing damage. These cords or rags must be discarded.

You cannot cross the road with the deceased, according to popular belief, as tumors will form on the body. When saying good-bye, you should not step on the towel placed near the coffin, so as not to curse yourself. These towels and cords that are used to lower the coffin must be left there and not pulled out.

Sometimes people may throw live flowers behind a coffin so that they step on them. Do not let them. In doing so, they are causing damage.

After you visit the cemetery, be sure to wash your hands. At wakes, you must not drink from a glass that was left out for the deceased, even if someone suggests doing it. If you do, you can get sick for a long time.

If you are digging or planting flowers near a grave and encounter some strange objects, you must burn them in the cemetery, trying not to breathe in or be touched by the smoke. If you know that one of your friends is coming to visit you directly from a funeral, do not let them into the house.

If you attend a funeral procession, men must take off their hats and quietly cross themselves. This should be done not only as a sign of respect but also for one's own health.

Russian peoples consider the dirt from the cemetery to be very dangerous. For example, people are so careful not to bring it home that those who dig graves are forced to strip and shake the dirt out of their shoes; none of the members of the household dare to touch it.

RADONITSA

Radonitsa is a spring pagan holiday of the Eastern Slavs associated with the cult of the ancestors. The name of the holiday comes from the words *kin* and *joy* and symbolizes honor for the memory of deceased relatives. In ancient times it was believed that on certain days of the year the souls of the deceased could return to their native places and even affect the lives of the living in a certain way. The Slavs believed that the dead could influence the harvest and fertility of the earth from their place in the underworld. When paganism was more prevalent, people would go to cemeteries at dawn on March 1 and give offerings to the deceased. The Slavs believed that the souls of the dead would rejoice at these activities.

Remnants of holidays that honor the dead are still preserved in many Slavic lands. The following tradition, like the custom of leaving food on a hill for one's ancestors, has existed for more than sixteen centuries. People take wine and food to the graves of their great-grandfathers (for the most part, they bring pancakes as symbols of the sun) and arrange calls (lamentations) and merrymaking (games, songs, and dances). The older members of the family return home after the ceremony, but the young people gather to dance, play games, and sing songs.

After Christianity was adopted, the church chose to recognize this custom. The pagan festival of radonitsa became organically "intertwined" with Orthodox Church traditions. The date became tied with the already-existing Passover in the church calendar, like most Orthodox holidays with pagan roots. This holiday takes a special place

Fig. 9.3. A radonitsa gathering in 2014. The Christian Church blesses the pagan ceremony of bringing food to the dead. Photograph by Perohanych.

among other church holidays, as it is considered the Passover of the departed. After the baptism of Russia it was celebrated during Fomin's week, which began on the first Sunday after Easter or on the following Tuesday (the latter is especially common).

CUSTOMS AND OMENS FOR RADONITSA

In the old days, people thought that the deceased visited their homes during radonitsa. They would put cups of water on the windowsill and three extra plates on the table where they had breakfast, lunch, and dinner in honor of their deceased relatives. They also heated the bathhouse and left clean clothes in it for the deceased to use. After that, they did not enter the bath or bathe for that day. On radonitsa, people would also prepare food and hand it out to the needy in honor of the deceased.

The main ritual people would perform on radonitsa was a call for rain. They believed that rain on radonitsa promised a rich harvest. Therefore, children would wait all day, calling for the rain to fall. If it did, they would bathe in the rainwater for luck.

When rain fell without thunder, girls would use the rainwater to wash their rings, whether silver or gold, believing that it would help to preserve their beauty and youth.

It was considered a bad omen to be engaged in agricultural work

Fig. 9.4. A family eats together at a cemetery in St. Petersburg, 1919.

that day. Sowing, digging, planting, and so on were all forbidden. Those who did such work ensured that they would have a meager and poor harvest.

Work was only allowed on radonitsa in the morning. All the work had to be finished by lunchtime. Then, the whole family would go to the cemetery to honor the deceased and join in the festivities in the evening.

WORKING WITH THE DEAD: SORCERY IN THE CEMETERY

Christianity gave the world a new character—the devil, which began to be associated with the gods of previous religions; for example, Saturn (his way of death with a scythe was most convenient) and Hecate (as the mistress of the cemetery in the new magical interpretation). Both Hecate and Saturn are ancient archetypal images that fit appropriately into the structure of the magical ritual but are not the personifications of evil. A huge mistake of modern new age believers is that they have, in fact, a partial Christian worldview; that is, a belief in absolute evil and in the dead as demons. As Eliphas Levi once wrote, "Man created a god in his own image and likeness!"

Sorcerers perform a considerable number of their rites in cemeteries. Cemeteries are strong places of power. Sorcerers who are going to the cemetery to work their sorcery observe certain rules even on the way to the cemetery. Once they enter the cemetery, they speak certain words and make a small offering in greeting. Once they are on cemetery land, sorcerers will continue to show deference and make offerings to the mistress and master of the cemetery. Common people are gradually losing their fear of sorcery in the cemetery.

Sorcerers treat the cemetery and all who rest there with great respect. Not all graves are suitable for sorcery. Only active graves in which the dead lie are able to fulfill a sorcerer's needs.

When they visit the cemetery, sorcerers carefully fasten all the buckles and buttons on their clothes and sorceresses carefully tie their hair. In addition, sorceresses try not to visit the cemeteries during their period if possible. Experienced sorcerers are able to choose the right grave for their work without difficulty by relying on their "vision." Beginners usually choose active graves according to certain signs or hints (although experienced spellcasters sometimes use the same signs).

Active Graves

An active grave attracts animals and birds. Watch to find out which graves birds sit on or circle frequently, whether they be crows, magpies, or other birds. This is a clear sign of activity.

Cats and dogs also like to wander near active graves. One of the best signs of a grave's activity is a cat sitting atop it. Sometimes there are dead trees on or next to an active grave. Often, trees on or near such a grave grow in crooked, ugly shapes. In the summer, vegetation withers, the grass is yellow and dry, and plants of any kind are reluctant to grow on an active grave. In winter, the snow that covers an active grave will appear crushed and gray. Watch for tracks left by animals and birds. If you can see the tracks of cats, dogs, or birds, or even the feathers of birds, then the grave is suitable for work. Watch for the movement of trees. The swaying of crowns and branches can indicate an active grave.

The gravestones at active graves can have many cracks and natural wear. The portraits on such graves fade faster and lose their brightness more quickly. Their crosses rot very quickly and very often break and fall. Malicious weeds usually grow well on active graves. The graves of children, young people, suicides, murder victims, and priests are often very suitable for use in sorcery. Family graves are often effective for sending death to someone you hate and inflicting madness.

As you walk between the graves, if you feel an oppressive atmosphere near a particular grave or if it makes you uncomfortable, this is also a sign of activity. After you have chosen a grave for your sorcery, stand next to it. Hold out your left palm and ask the inhabitant of the grave if he agrees to do what you ask. Use great focus and concentration, guided by your senses, when you ask. If you feel a quiet heat or tingling in the palm of your hand, then this grave is suitable. If you feel cold, emptiness, anxiety, or fear, continue your search. If there is suddenly a strong wind, it begins to rain, or you begin to feel oppressive discomfort or fear, you should stop searching. This is a sign that the owners of the cemetery reject you.

Once you have found a suitable grave, greet the deceased. Depending on the ritual you are performing, you may also give an offering to the dead either before or after the rite. In modern times, sorcerers and sorceresses use silver coins, expensive tobacco products, strong spirits, sweets (honey, etc.), blood sacrifices (preferably black roosters, less often hens and young chickens), and rarely, gold and other jewelry for such greetings and offerings. Of course, blood sacrifices are the best offering. Sorcerers do not use rice, millet, breadcrumbs, or bread, as these simply graze the inhabitant of the grave; they do not send him to work. Also, do not use a premade supply of blood and meat as offerings. The energy of the blood comes out when the victim is sacrificed. After this brief moment, the blood is simply liquid and the meat is just meat.

Sorcerers and sorceresses work not only at graves in the cemeteries but also at the cemetery crossroads. Sorcerers give their offerings and greetings directly to Death when they go to the cemetery crossroads. Less often, sorcerers conduct rituals at cemetery fences, trees, and the like. After they complete a ritual, sorcerers and sorceresses leave the cemetery, saying special words as they cross its border and observing certain rules until they reach the very threshold of their home. After they return from the cemetery, sorcerers perform special procedures to cleanse themselves.

All conjurers perform the ritual in honor of Death at least once a year. The sorcerers prepare an offering in advance and go to the cemetery once the sun has set to perform this rite.

Much of the work sorcerers and sorceresses do takes place in forests. It is believed that the devil sometimes likes to be in the forest. When sorcerers enter forestland to perform sorcery, they give greetings and appropriate offerings. It is strictly forbidden to litter on forestland. A sorcerer is also not allowed to cut down trees or bushes without first making a formal request or giving the corresponding offerings. All sorcerers and sorceresses love walking through the forest, cleansing themselves of any accumulated fatigue and drinking in the natural power that emanates from it.

The cemetery, the "city of the dead," has the following topography. There are Portals, Gates Big and Small (that is, the central entrance and additional entryways); there is a Wall, a Fence, a perimeter that separates the world of the living from the world of the dead; and there is the graveyard itself, with its crossroads, named and unnamed graves, chapels, and other altars. When a sorcerer works in a cemetery, he plunges into Dark Waters, moves to another reality, to the Lower World, completely altering consciousness. Such a displacement of the departure point allows you to quickly connect to the required energy, pass it through yourself, and direct it to achieve your goals. Otherwise, without immersion in a trance, any magical action turns into the cheapest show, at the level of a common disco. The sorcerer is like a catcher of pearls who dives into the abyss of the sea holding his breath, and it is up to him whether he will come up with rich prey or stay at the bottom.

Since sorcery is inextricably linked with visiting and working with graveyards, here are the rules and subtleties for visiting cemeteries. I see that in many books people talk about working with the dead, but they never say how or what you should do, and this is a very important part.

Required Actions

- You must show care and respect (to the dead and death in general, to cemetery entities and forces, and of course, to the master of the cemetery), for these are the forces to which we turn, and who help us.
- We do not shy away from providing maintenance at the grave chosen for work: we must fix flowers and remove dirt, rubbish, dry leaves, etc.
- Maintain calmness, concentration, and detachment. You should not feel nervous, depressed or distracted, afraid, or feel remorse for the deed; avoid uncertainty, doubts, and excessive impressionability.

Activities That Are Not Allowed

- Noise, extraneous sources of sound (mobile phones, music players, etc.), loud conversations, whistles.

- Visiting the cemetery under the influence of drugs or alcohol.
- Leaving behind garbage, cigarette butts; defiling the graves; any actions that may show disrespect for local "inhabitants."
- Taking something away from the graveyard, except for rituals in which the removal of items for further sorcery use is negotiated separately (in this case, follow the instructions from the rite).

When You Go to the Graveyard

- Go through the gate. Before entering, stop, bow slightly, give a greeting in your own words or, for example, "I bow to the kingdom of the dead, respect and honor to you," to express your respect. Explain the purpose of your visit.
- Begin to search for the "right" grave for your works (an erroneous choice will destroy your efforts). A grave can be either active or extinct. You will need an active one (see below).

Signs of an Active Grave

- Animal traces (birds and their feathers, dogs, cats). Animals are more sensitive to such manifestations than humans; therefore, in this case they can serve as good indicators.
- Poor, sluggish vegetation; withered grass; unusual or dried-up trees; nettle.
- Your inner sensations.
- Gravestones or crosses are easily broken on active graves. They may have cracks and worn or faded carving.
- You can use the presence of an anthill in the cemetery territory; the grave to the left of the anthill (as you face it) is active.

Some Considerations When Choosing Graves

- Children's graves (up to twelve years of age) are effective for rituals of love or gambling, but such tombs should only be worked by experienced masters; this is very dangerous!
- A grave with a sagging cross is effective for sending diseases and ill health.

- A grave in which more than three members of a family rest is effective for sending madness.
- The ninth grave from the entrance to the churchyard is effective for a deadly curse.
- A grave in the far-left corner of the cemetery is effective for a heavy/deadly curse.

Greeting the Deceased and Execution of Magical Work

- Verbally ask for forgiveness for disturbing them. State the request with which you came. You don't need to have brilliant linguistic abilities to do so.
- At the grave, sprinkle a pinch of dried black bread.
- If you want to please the deceased especially, you can start the ritual with three small lit candles (unless in the description of the ritual there are special instructions to this effect).

Performing the Ritual

- Perform it in accordance with the way it is described. Know all the texts from it by heart.
- After the completion of the rite, leave offerings.

Leaving the Graveyard

- Leave by a different route (do not exit through the same gate).
- Say good-bye in your own words and thank them for their help (mentally).
- So that nothing "clings" (essence, for example) say the following: "There are ties that call me, and so I have a home beyond. Amen." Or you could say: "Dead with the dead, living with the living. You remain here, but I must return home."
- Do not look back under any circumstances.
- Go home in absolute silence.
- Do not tell anyone at all about what has been done.
- Clean yourself and your clothes and shoes.

HOW A GRAVEYARD SPELL WORKS

Sorcery at the cemetery does not cause harm to experienced sorceresses. The sorceress invokes the spirit of a dead person and asks that spirit to attach magical power to the person being worked on, to weaken the resisting soul so the spell will work with tremendous power. The necessary effect of the ritual comes when the person being worked on is in a weakened state after stress, a quarrel, divorce, or illness. The spell takes on great power and works for many years, and its action cannot be removed with the help of bright magic or church prayers.

Usually these rituals are performed during a waxing or full moon and begin to affect the actions of a person within a week or even just a few days. You can call on spirits or demons (for a quicker effect), but it is not always possible to make a dark entity obey. Many demons love to be naughty, so they must be restrained to make sure they do no harm to any of the living. For example, you may be working on a request to connect a man with his beloved wife who has left the family, but in doing so the demons play a joke and deprive the man of a child or relative. To prevent this from happening, sorceresses and warlocks give the owner of the cemetery a gift or ransom payment.

A graveyard spell leaves a strong trail on a person's karma, whether it is love or curse, or money or job sorcery.

CROSSROADS IN THE CEMETERY

As we have discussed, important places of power for sorcerers are the crossroads of roads and paths. The crossroads has been considered a place with magical powers for centuries. The forces of Unholy Power love crossroads; therefore, crossroads are places of unique power. People have long been making deals with demons at crossroads, appealing to the gods, and giving offerings. At the symbolic level, a crossroads is the intersection of four elements that provides balance and at the same time acts as a gateway to the otherworld. At the crossroads, there is a meeting of the four sides of the world. You can perform many works of magic at a crossroads, including the removal of curses and spells. Sorcerers will also visit crossroads for specific purposes related to the remnants of a sorcerous work. This can include the act of self-cleansing.

For some particularly important sorcerous actions (such as initiations, contracts, and the like), a sorcerer will search fields, deserts, and glades for a place where three dirt roads intersect (that is, a crossroads that diverges on six sides). Among sorcerers, this kind of crossroads is called the devil's cross, and it is a strong place of power. It is believed that the devil not only likes to visit such crossroads but also listens to the requests and wishes of sorcerers and sorceresses who perform their works there. Occasionally, a ceremony will involve even more complex crossroads (four roads and more). When they arrive at the crossroads, the sorcerers greet the devil and give him offerings (this list is essentially the same as the one for graveyard offerings).

The dirt from any crossroads can be cursed and spelled, but a cemetery crossroads is even more powerful. At the cemetery crossroads you are dealing not with four elements but with five, because the energy of death, or Necro, is added to the energy of the crossroads. At the cemetery crossroads, you can call to the dead and they will certainly respond to your call. Demons will also come to your call. They are called the seventh legion of demons.

In the next section I will tell you about sorcerous works in the cemetery, some of which involve a cemetery crossroads.

CEMETERY SPELLS

❊ Curse at Cemetery Crossroads

At the center of a cemetery crossroads, draw a triangle with an aspen stick. Make each side about a foot long. Draw equilateral crosses along the sides of the triangle.

Take dirt from a grave that is immediately to the left of the cemetery entrance and pour it into the center of the triangle.

Walk around the triangle with the pile of dirt at its center three times counterclockwise and say:

> *By the dark streams of misfortunes and troubles,*
> *By the dark streams of sorrow and tears,*

By the cold breath of the dead,
And the groaning of the grave,
Let a curse enter this dirt.
Let it cause evil to [name of your enemy],
It is [name of your enemy] that I want to kill.
By the power of those who are buried here
He will be destroyed.
Let it be so!

After you say the words *Let it be so!* stick the aspen stick directly into the pile of dirt in the center of the triangle. Collect the dirt in a pouch made of dark cloth. Then use it to guide your curse. Pour it out near your enemy's doorstep or someplace he will be likely to step on it.

This cursed dirt is much stronger than simple grave dirt.

❋ A Very Strong Curse

To perform this curse, a sorcerer must get the tibia of a hanged man.

In the Middle Ages the corpses on the gallows hung until the birds completely picked off all the flesh, and then the bones lay under the gallows. It was there that the sorcerer could pick up the tibia and return home.

The sorcerer would put the bone on an altar and read "Our Father" over it nine times, backward and in Latin:

Nema Olam a son arebil des menoitatnet ni sacudni son en te. Sirtson subiotibed sumittimid son te tucis, artson atibed sibon ettimid te. Eidoh sibon ad munaiditouq murtson menap. Arreta ni oleac ni tucis, aut satnulov taif muut munger tainevda. Muut nemon rutecifitcnas, sileac ni se iuq retson retap.

Then the sorcerer appealed to the spirit of the deceased:

Come through the noose, come over death's threshold. Let the power of the dark release you to find your way back through the noose. Come and do my work [the sorcerer explained his request, usually to kill a person or a whole family].

The sorcerer used ink to write his request on the bone, as well.

After the ink was dry, he buried the bone for three days at a cemetery crossroads, saying:

Take this power through the land where Death dwells.

Three days later, the sorcerer would return to the place he buried the bone and dig it up. He would slaughter a black chicken and let its blood drain directly onto the bone in the pit.

Then the sorcerer would hold the bloody bone in his hands and say:

Carry this curse to those for whom I have no love.

He would bury the chicken and the bone in the same grave and go away without ever looking back. Usually he buried these bones near the victim's house or attempted to place it in either the foundation or the wall of the house.

The people who lived in houses near the buried bones would usually begin to go crazy. Such people had the unfortunate honor of always hearing noises and seeing objects move and fall untouched. They observed what today is called a poltergeist.

❊ Healing at a Cemetery Crossroads

The cemetery crossroads and the force that it contains can be used not only to harm but also to heal a hopelessly sick or accursed person.

If a person is very sick and cannot get well, let them go to an old cemetery and find a crossroads there. At the center of the crossroads, they must recite the following spell:

The power of silence lurks in Death
Cleanse me from filth,
Cleanse me of the evil eye,
Cleanse me of the sorceress's words,
Cleanse me of the sorcerer's deeds.
Let the boat to the other world pass by,
Let my illness go away,
Quiet the power that touches me.
I'll go to my grave

At the time written in Death's ledger.
But that time has not come,
And I will live in health.
Let it be so.

The spell must be read thirteen times. After that, the petitioner must find a grave of someone with the same name and bury one of their own possessions there. While doing so, they must say:

I do not bury my possession here but leave my illness,
Forever and ever, by names long forgotten, I call upon you,
O grave, to take this illness from me for all time!
Let it be so!

The person must leave without turning around to look back. If the grave takes on the disease, then the person will soon recover.

❋ Spell to Alter an Unfortunate Fate

There are people who are born unhappy, with constant failures and problems. But you can get rid of bad karma.

Those who are haunted by misfortunes and troubles must go to the cemetery at midnight during a full moon and find a crossroads. In the center of the crossroads, draw a triangle. Draw it with an aspen stick. Dig a fairly deep pit in the triangle.

Put something of your own in the pit. Cut off the head of a white hen over the pit and, while the blood drips over your possession, read the following spell:

Through death and the souls of the dead, I renounce my fate.
Through the tomb of the forgotten and the nameless, I renounce my share of misfortune.
With the blood of the victim, I repay my fate.
Through the cemetery, through the grave, through the tombstone,
I call upon the Witness.
As the blood goes into the earth, so will my fate change in my favor.
Let it be so!

Throw the chicken in the pit, fill in the hole, and leave without looking back at any point.

❊ Get Rid of a Spouse's Lover

Go to a cemetery, find a grave with the same name as your rival, take a handful of dirt from it, and go to a river. Throw the dirt in the river three times and say the following charm against a rival:

As this dead man lies in his grave,
And from his coffin and grave does not escape,
So my husband [or wife] will not leave me
To [name of the rival].
The deceased goes to the grave, the coffin goes to the grave.
The grave of a dead man in the earth,
And you, [spouse's name], come to me,
To your wife [or husband].
As the river continues to flow,
Escapes the shore banks,
So [name of the rival]
From [name of spouse] will go forever.
There are no ways to find him [or her].
And until the dirt is returned to the grave
Until then, my charm will not break.
Forever and ever.
Amen. Amen. Amen.

Do this on a waning moon, in the evening by a river with a rapid current. The faster the river the faster they will part. Read the charms three times and leave an offering on the grave.

❊ Love Spell

For this rite, three fresh marked graves are needed. On each of them carry out the following actions: First, place an offering (kutya, pancakes, red wine). Then light a candle and hold it in your hand. Put the photo of your beloved on the grave, and let it lie there while you read:

The late [name], I bow to you, I remember you, I call out your spirit.
I leave you an offering, I call upon [name].
Go to the field, go to the forest, the quicksand, the rotten log where I swam,
Find [name of beloved]. Take away his heart, put in him the mortal grief of [name of beloved].
As your whole family cries for you, mourns, so the heart of [name of beloved] for [your name] hurts.
As the fish on the shore dies without water, the grass dries without earth-mother, the sky does not exist without clouds,
So let [name of beloved] never forget [your name].
As the candle burns, so [name of beloved] from love for [your name] is consumed.
And who will treat it will become tired from the first day.
Amen.

Read this three times. After the last reading, put the candle on the grave. Bury the photo at the foot of the grave with the following words:

Late [name], tie [name of beloved] with your cross, tombstone, cemetery fence to [your name]. Without her, he will fall to the ghouls, and with her, he will find happiness. So be it.

❊ Another Love Spell

Three days before the date scheduled for the rite, buy two bouquets of artificial flowers for the gravesite, two red candles, and a long black ribbon.

Also, go to the cemetery and find a common family grave where a husband and wife are lying; do this in advance so as not to spend a long time searching when you perform the rite. The names of the deceased are not important. This is where the main part of the rite will be held.

During these three days, you must put three candles under the cross in three different churches, with the following words:

The cross of the church, the cross of sorrow, as people came to you with tears, so cry for me, shed tears for me. Her heart has been

> *filled with love, her body has been scorched by lust. As a candle burns out, so let [name] lose her mind for me. May it be so!*

On the way out, say:

> *As hunters, I'll be glad to hunt up to the money, and [name] will be good for me. May it be so!*

On the third day immediately after visiting the church, take the bouquets, the ribbon, and the two candles to the cemetery to the chosen gravesite. Put the bouquets on it and light the candles.

Use the black ribbon to tightly bind the two headstones, or crosses, and tie it into a knot. Then get up so that the resulting knot is in front of you, take the candles in your hands, and, dropping melting wax on it three times, read the following charm three times:

> *I'm standing in a cemetery, between two graves, old graves, but bound by strong bonds. Nobody ever tore these knots in life, and after death, even more so.*

❊ A Curse

Take forty nails, and say over each:

> *It is not with a nail that I punish [name], but with the sting of demons.*
> *Demons will have [name]'s blood to drink,*
> *His meat to guzzle, his soul to tear with their claws.*

After you have cursed the nails, take them and a photo of the enemy, find a big stump in the forest, and attach the photo to it with the cursed nails. As you pound in the nails, read over each one:

> *O demons!*
> *Go into the open field,*
> *In the dense forest, to the damp stump.*
> *There he, [name], is waiting.*
> *Devour his soul, body, blood.*
> *Do not let him live, send him to his grave.*
> *Do not let him have a family, but let him be alone.*
> *Amen. Amen. Amen.*

After you pin the photo to the stump, fill the stump with forty handfuls of dirt from the grave of someone with the victim's name. (Gather the dirt in advance.)

Then put a candle in the dirt on the stump and read forty times:

> *As this candle burns, so the charmed [name] will die away. Amen.*

Leave silently, without looking back.

❋ Curse to Cause Poverty

Perform this curse during the waning moon at sunset. As the work is carried out in the cemetery, observe all the rules of cemetery work. Find a grave with the name of the enemy and bury three coins, preferably pennies, at the foot of the grave and say the following thirteen times:

> *As for a dead man, no money is needed, so [name], will not see a single penny. Amen.*

After three days, dig up and discard the coins at the enemy's home outside the door.

❋ Punishment of Enemy

During the waning moon, at sunset, go to the cemetery and find an old, abandoned, unmarked grave and bury the possession of an enemy while saying the following words (read three times):

> *Dead man, all forgotten, as you look at the light alone, so [name] will live alone in the world without light.*
> *No one will look at him or miss him, neither friends nor family, so that [name] did not know any friends, everyone turned their faces away from him, did not help him, did not call him, did not visit him.*
> *Cover the grave with soil, so that everyone will forget it.*
> *They will not greet it, but bypass it, everyone and everything, women and men, young men and old people, young and mischievous, relatives and strangers, to all of them will [name] be forgotten, forgotten, forgotten, and never mourned. Amen.*

Remember to observe the rules of work in the cemetery.

❊ Spell to Break Up a Couple

Take dirt from graves with the names of the people you want to break up, leaving an offering on each grave in return. Take two photos of the people to be broken up and sew them together with their backs to each other using black thread. Pour grave dirt between them. As you do so, read the following charm:

I conjure, I command, [names] forever I tear asunder,
There is a world between them, and it is as cold as the grave.
Heart will not grow with heart, but heart from heart will be turned away.
On the ninth day there will be a chill,
On the fortieth a bad scandal,
And in a year all love will be gone.
I dissuade them with dark words and grave dirt,
So that they will not be together and will not live together, will not love, will not bear children.
It is said, woven, done.
May it be so!

Bury the resulting packet at a cemetery crossroads. Do not forget about the rules of working in the cemetery.

❊ Spell to Make a Debtor Pay

Buy a white candle and flowers. Go to a cemetery and find an untended gravestone marked with the same name as the debtor. Put everything in order, then place a lighted candle and flowers on the gravestone. Put a coin under the flowers and say:

[Name of the deceased], as you live in heaven, you know more about earthly concerns. Guide [name of the debtor], who is in debt to me, to return what I have given him without delay. I have need, but not for enemies. I'll remember you; I will not forget about your help. Amen.

And very soon you will see your debtor, and all your money will be returned.

10

Simple Tips for All Occasions

Never pick up coins in the street and do not take them from the hands of your enemies or people who envy you. Money is a powerful magic tool and a charm that can seriously affect your life.

You cannot wash a mirror while thinking about a dead person. The mirror can become a portal to the world of the dead. If you have made this mistake, then cover it with a black rag and turn it to face the wall for seven days. This will help to avoid trouble.

Be wary of someone else's car that holds the energy of the previous owner. This energy can negatively affect the new owner. If you buy a car from someone else, you must perform a rite of purification.

A dream in which you kill a person or cause them suffering and pain really creates the opposite effect. In fact, it means that this person is a threat to you. You should stay away from them.

Do not give promises to those who are dying. If you do not fulfill them, it can lead to very terrible consequences.

The otherworld constantly gives us signs. It is important to be able to listen and hear them. The sign can be anything: a dream, a hiccup on the street, a sound heard accidentally, a smell, a picture. You have to listen to everything that surrounds you. It will help you to avoid trouble, make the right choices, and improve your life.

If you constantly hear the same melody, it is a sign that very soon your life will change.

If you want to bind a person to yourself, then give them the same keychain or bracelet that you have. The same trinkets will keep two people's energy intertwined.

Try not to allow your ill-wishers to get your blood. Blood is used in the most terrible magical rites.

Meeting with a person on a doorstep or stairs leads to trouble. You cannot get acquainted with anyone on the stairs or doorstep. This can lead to quarrels, disagreements, and misfortunes.

Keeping medicines near the bed can lead to a serious illness. When we get sick, the medications ease our condition and help fight the disease, but later the medicine packaging acquires the energy of the disease and draws out our vitality.

Unmarried girls cannot have a cat in the house until they have a dating life. If a single girl gets a cat in her house, she may stay alone for long time and never get married. Cats feel the energy of people and are able to influence it. If a cat feels threatened by a man who comes into the house to her mistress, then she can energetically affect him, and the relationship of such a couple will collapse.

You cannot keep house flowers in cracked pots. A cracked flowerpot leads to quarrels and scandals in the family.

A girl cannot wear her young man's shirt. Wearing your beloved's clothes is dangerous, as it can lead to you losing that love forever.

To keep children's photos together with official documents is a bad omen. You can lose the emotional connection with the child forever and destroy their life.

Elderly people should never be allowed to sleep with young children; vital energy flows freely during sleep, so an elderly person can unknowingly consume the energy of the child.

Be careful if a person suddenly starts to focus persistent attention on you and patiently persevere. Their thoughts may be unclean. Do not share any plans, desires, emotions, or things of any kind with them. Try not to allow them to take any of your hair.

Try not to give alms (money, most often) to homeless people. They can send evil or damnation your way.

Do not buy vintage jewelry without knowing its history. Furthermore, do not take it from the dead.

It is dangerous to buy things that someone once wore, because they contain the energy of the past owner. If this energy turns out to be negative, then the life of the new owner will be hurt.

You cannot take pictures with people you do not like. A part of your soul will always remain next to a person with whom you have a negative relationship, which can negatively affect your whole life. Take pictures only with those who wish you well and love you.

To store pictures of the dead with pictures of living people is a bad omen. The energy of the deceased can be transmitted to living people. Create a separate album for pictures of those who are no longer alive.

Do not take pictures if you are sick, tired, or do not look well. The state will remain the same in the picture, which can harm your energy.

Do not take pictures too often in your home. Such photos make you very vulnerable to curses and the evil eye. Select a neutral background for a photo session.

Do not give your pictures out unrestrainedly. There are many cases when a curse has been cast on such a photo. A person can also tear up your photo or just throw it away, which will also adversely affect your health.

Do not store photos in your wallet. They do not belong there. According to popular wisdom, pictures put into a wallet will negatively affect the financial well-being as well as the health of the person depicted in the photo. Photos and wallets have completely different energies. Do not mix them.

You cannot take anything given by strangers. This can lead to unexpected consequences.

In the days of the summer solstice you should not engage in creative work: do not build or repair structures and buildings, create any objects (with the exception of sorcery tools and ritual supplies), sculpt jugs, weave, darn, or knit.

A daughter must not cut her mother's hair. This is a bad omen and will lead to quarrels.

You cannot share a bag with anyone, otherwise everything in your life will have to be divided in half.

You cannot celebrate birthdays at a party, either at your home or at another person's home, otherwise everything in life can change radically. You will give your luck and success away by celebrating birthdays.

If a loved one gives you a ring as a token of engagement and it slips out of your hand, this is a bad sign; there will be no wedding.

Do not put pillows on the table. You will attract great trouble.

You cannot celebrate your birthday in advance, otherwise the whole year you will be haunted by problems.

You cannot introduce your significant other to a friend on a Tuesday. Otherwise, he or she may become the second person in your relationship (i.e., a lover).

If you keep empty pails at home, then a close friend may deceive you. You must stack buckets on top of each other and place something in the topmost bucket before putting them away.

When you are settling into a new house or apartment (it doesn't matter whether you are buying or renting), you cannot replace your slippers for a whole year, otherwise you will have to replace the person you love.

You cannot wear a hostess's slippers in her house, otherwise the hostess will kick you out of her house, even though she may not wish to. It is important to have several pairs of house shoes available to guests.

If a child purchases clothes that he will grow into, he may become a parent early.

Scissors are one of the most magical items. They are often used in spells and sorcery. Scissors are made of metal, which has the strongest mystical properties. Therefore, you must be very careful with scissors. First, you should not give them away; second, if you drop them, you must stand on them with your right foot, and only then pick them up, otherwise you will experience misfortune. You can also use scissors to protect yourself. If you open them in the shape of a cross and place them on your threshold, they will prevent bad people, envious people, and enemies from entering your house.

You cannot give men stuffed animals, as this makes them vulnerable. If you have already given a toy to them, make sure that the toy does not fall into the wrong hands.

A bride must wear new things for the wedding, because old things will act as homewreckers. They will not only destroy the wedding but also destroy her family life.

You cannot photograph a sleeping person, or you will deprive them of life force.

You cannot clean the house after sunset, or you will repel your family and friends.

If you are given a figure of an elephant with a lowered trunk, either do not take it or return it to the presenter. Such an elephant can bring misfortune to your home.

Each member of a family cannot have their own personal cup, as this leads to discord in the family.

Husband and wife cannot sleep under different blankets, as this leads to a cooling of relations and divorce. If you still plan to sleep that way, you should put a skein of white threads under the mattress.

If you speak over a threshold, you will be caught up in a quarrel. Do not say hello and do not talk to anyone over the doorstep. Otherwise, you may quarrel strongly or part with this person.

You cannot cut your hair yourself, for you will cut your own happiness, your relationship will go wrong, and you will have frequent quarrels.

If your heel breaks, you will stumble in life. If you have a broken heel before making an important decision, you should wait. This is a warning. Consider everything once again.

Children under six cannot be taken to the cemetery, otherwise the woes of the most recently deceased relative will pass to the family of the child.

If you are pregnant, you cannot accept gifts for a child who has not yet been born. Something may happen to both the mother and the child.

To keep a pregnancy, you cannot sing a lullaby to a still unborn child.

Index

About the Author

Natasha Helvin is an occultist, hereditary witch, and priestess in the traditional Caribbean religion as well as an avid scholar of tradition and religion. She was born and raised in the Soviet state until she was eighteen. She inherited her passion for magic and fortune-telling from her mother and previous generations. She learned from her family the ancient secrets of magic and healing and the boundless potential of the human spirit. From this long line of metaphysicians and her rich spiritual cultural heritage, the roots of occultism and conscious thinking developed in her rapidly and at a very young age. As a child, she saw her grandmother and mother use magic in their everyday lives to help neighbors, friends, and anyone simply seeking help.

As a passionate traveler, Natasha loves various magical practices of ancient cultures and civilizations. The introduction of a powerful combination of modern methods of the mind into various forms of cultural magic has become a significant part of her personal practice, and this is what she shares with her clients.

Her passion for methods aimed at manifestation and the practical use of real sorcery has always been at the forefront of her life. Natasha Helvin's life goal is to share this practical, time-tested knowledge of sorcery with those who are looking for an alternative way and want to get a little more out of life. She is firmly convinced that we are in our physical body to experience the physical reality to the fullest. This means living a luxurious life, creating a successful business, and simply enjoying a happy, healthy family. Life must be amazing, and we create it ourselves!

Natasha prefers the more intense side of sorcery. She likes to go beyond the bounds of the accessible and prefers the magic of strong influence, relationship spells, and various forms of spiritual manipulation. Customers go to Natasha for her unique spells and counseling. With these, she gives people new perspectives and the kind of experience that leads to true life changes and long-term results.